Technology and Innovation Policy

NEW HORIZONS IN INNOVATION MANAGEMENT

Books in the New Horizons in Innovation Management series make a significant contribution to the development of Innovation Studies. As this field has expanded dramatically in recent years, the series will provide an invaluable forum for the publication of high-quality works of scholarship and show the diversity of issues and practices around the world.

Global in its approach, it includes some of the best theoretical and empirical work with contributions to fundamental principles, rigorous evaluations of existing concepts and competing theories, historical surveys and future visions.

Titles in the series include:

Responsible Innovation in Digital Health
Empowering the Patient
Edited by Tatiana Iakovleva, Elin M. Oftedal and John Bessant

Technology Transfer and US Public Sector Innovation
Albert N. Link and Zachary T. Oliver

Innovation Management
Perspectives from Strategy, Product, Process and Human Resource Research
Edited by Vida Škudienė, Jason Li-Ying and Fabian Bernhard

Defense Technological Innovation
Issues and Challenges in an Era of Converging Technologies
Bharat Rao, Adam Jay Harrison and Bala Mulloth

Organizational Innovation
Theory, Research, and Direction
Fariborz Damanpour

Technology and Innovation Policy
An International Perspective
James A. Cunningham and Albert N. Link

Technology and Innovation Policy

An International Perspective

James A. Cunningham

Professor of Strategic Management, Newcastle Business School, Northumbria University, UK

Albert N. Link

Virginia Batte Phillips Distinguished Professor of Economics, University of North Carolina at Greensboro, USA

NEW HORIZONS IN INNOVATION MANAGEMENT

Cheltenham, UK • Northampton, MA, USA

Published by
Edward Elgar Publishing Limited
The Lypiatts
15 Lansdown Road
Cheltenham
Glos GL50 2JA
UK

Edward Elgar Publishing, Inc.
William Pratt House
9 Dewey Court
Northampton
Massachusetts 01060
USA

A catalogue record for this book
is available from the British Library

Library of Congress Control Number: 2021938821

This book is available electronically in the **Elgar**online
Business subject collection
http://dx.doi.org/10.4337/9781789902891

Printed on elemental chlorine free (ECF)
recycled paper containing 30% Post-Consumer Waste

ISBN 978 1 78990 288 4 (cased)
ISBN 978 1 78990 289 1 (eBook)

Printed and bound in the USA

For Sammi, Aiden, and Riley

For Carol

Contents

List of figures viii
List of tables xii
About the authors xv
Acknowledgements xviii
List of abbreviations xix

1 Technology and innovation policy: setting the stage 1

2 Technology policies to enhance private-sector R&D 15

3 The effectiveness of technology policy 45

4 Unanticipated consequences of technology policy 52

5 The technology policy environment 75

6 Technology policies to leverage public-sector R&D 93

7 Global innovation systems 118

8 Toward a technology/innovation policy ecosystem 126

References 133
Index 146

Figures

1.1 Annual percentage change in U.K. Gross Domestic Product per capita in constant prices 10

1.2 Annual percentage change in U.S. Gross Domestic Product per capita in constant prices 10

1.3 Annual percentage change in G7 Gross Domestic Product per capita in constant prices 11

2.1 Gross domestic expenditures on R&D by U.K. firms in the private sector, U.S. $2015M and PPP 18

2.2 Gross domestic R&D performed in the U.K. private sector, U.S. $2015M and PPP 18

2.3 Gross domestic expenditures on R&D by U.S. firms in the private sector, U.S. $2015M and PPP 19

2.4 Gross domestic R&D performed in the U.S. private sector, U.S. $2015M and PPP 19

2.5 Gross domestic expenditures on R&D by G7 firms in the private sector, U.S. $2015M and PPP 20

2.6 Gross domestic R&D performed in the G7 private sector, U.S. $2015M and PPP 20

2.7 Multi-factor productivity growth index for the United Kingdom, years 1985–2018 24

2.8 Multi-factor productivity growth index for the United States, years 1985–2018 25

2.9 Growth in multi-factor productivity and the percent of gross domestic investments in R&D in the private sector for year 2017 for selected countries 28

2.10 The economics of an R&D tax incentive 37

3.1 Framework for explaining the role of investments in R&D and the role of technology policy and innovation policy in the economy 45

4.1 Framework for explaining the role of investments in R&D and the role of technology policy and innovation policy in the economy 54

4.2 Unanticipated consequences from a technology policy 55

4.3 Trend in number of Phase I SBIR awards and number of funded firms, by fiscal year 63

4.4 Trend in number of Phase II SBIR awards and number of funded firms, by fiscal year 64

4.5 Ratio of Phase II awards in year (t +1) to Phase I awards in year (t), by fiscal year 64

4.6 Trend in Phase I SBIR award amounts and obligated amounts for year 2015 forward, by fiscal year in current and constant $2015 65

4.7 Trend in Phase II SBIR award amounts and obligated amounts for year 2015 forward, by fiscal year in current and constant $2015 67

4.8 Ratio of cumulative Phase II awards to cumulative Phase I awards, by funding agency 68

4.9 Trend in Department of Defense Phase I SBIR award amounts and obligated amounts, by fiscal year in current and constant $2015 69

4.10 Trend in Department of Defense Phase II SBIR award amounts and obligated amounts, by fiscal year in current and constant $2015 69

4.11 Trend in Department of Health and Human Services Phase I SBIR award amounts and obligated amounts, by fiscal year in current and constant $2015 70

4.12 Trend in Department of Health and Human Services Phase II SBIR award amounts and obligated amounts, by fiscal year in current and constant $2015 70

5.1 Framework for explaining the role of investments in R&D and the role of technology policy and innovation policy in the economy 75

5.2 The economics of a patent system 79

5.3 Patent applications by United Kingdom and United States inventors to the European Patent Office (EPO) by inventor's country of residence, years 1978–2017 81

5.4 Patent applications by United Kingdom and United States inventors to the U.S. Patent and Trademark Office (USPTO) by inventor's country of residence, years 1995–2017 81

5.5 The economics of collaborative R&D 86

6.1 Gross domestic R&D performed in the U.K. academic sector, years 1981–2018, U.S. $2015M and PPP 96

6.2 Gross domestic R&D performed in the U.S. academic sector, years 1981–2018, U.S. $2015M and PPP 97

6.3 Percent of R&D performed in the academic sector for basic research and the percent of R&D performed in the academic sector funded by the government, by country, for year 2017 100

6.4 Cumulative proportion of countries with university-based technology transfer policies, years 1981–2010 113

6.5 U.S. university patent applications and patent awards, years 2000–2018 114

6.6 Framework for explaining the role of investments in R&D and the role of technology policy and innovation policy in the economy 116

7.1 Expanded framework for explaining the role of investments in R&D and the role of private-sector and public-sector technology policies 124

8.1 Framework for explaining the role of investments in R&D and the role of private-sector and public-sector technology policies with an emphasis on the technology policy environment 126

8.2 Framework for explaining the role of investments in R&D and the role of private-sector and public-sector technology policies expanded to include the technology policy ecosystem 127

Tables

1.1 Definitions of key terms 3

2.1 Mean percent of gross domestic R&D financed by firms in the private sector, by country and country groups, years 1981–2017 17

2.2 Percent of gross domestic R&D financed by firms in the private sector, by country for year 2017 21

2.3 Private-sector firm investments in R&D and R&D performed in the private sector, by country for year 2017, U.S. $2015M and PPP 23

2.4 Growth in multi-factor productivity and the percent of gross domestic R&D financed by firms in the private sector for year 2017 for selected countries 27

2.5 Percent of Gross Domestic Product allocated to selected technology policies, years 2016 and 2017 30

2.6 R&D tax incentive in the European Union, by country 32

2.7 Government support of private-sector firm R&D through tax incentives in year 2016 as a percentage of Gross Domestic Product, by country 36

2.8 Government support of private-sector firm R&D through direct subsidies as a percentage of Gross Domestic Product for year 2017, by country 39

2.9 Comparison of number of SBRI program awards in the United Kingdom and number of SBIR program awards in the United States 41

2.10 Comparison of award amounts of the SBRI program in the United Kingdom and the SBIR program awards in the United States (£ 000s) 42

2.11 International adoption of programs similar to the U.S. SBIR Program 42

3.1 Percent of gross domestic R&D financed by firms in the private sector, by country for year 2017 47

3.2 Government support of private-sector firm R&D through tax incentives for year 2016 as a percentage of Gross Domestic Product, by country 48

3.3 Government support of private-sector firm R&D through direct subsidies as a percentage of Gross Domestic Product for year 2017, by country 49

4.1 Phase I SBIR awards, by fiscal year 61

4.2 Phase II SBIR awards, by fiscal year 62

4.3 Cumulative number of Phase I SBIR awards and funded firms, by funding agency 66

4.4 Cumulative number of Phase II SBIR awards and funded firms, by funding agency 67

4.5 Distribution of Year 2014 Phase II awards, by SBIR funding agency 71

5.1 Patent applications to the European Patent Office and the U.S. Patent and Trademark Office by inventor's country of residence, year 2017 82

5.2 European Patent Office granted patents, top ten countries for years 2018 and 2019 83

5.3 Percent of R&D active and non-R&D active firms engaging in collaboration in innovation, by R&D status, years 2008–2010 88

5.4 Percent of product and/or process innovating firms collaborating on innovation with higher education or research institutions, by size, years 2012–2014 89

6.1 R&D performed in the academic sector, by country in year 2017, U.S. $2015M and PPP 98

6.2 R&D performed in the academic sector allocated to basic research for year 2017, U.S. $2015M and PPP 99

6.3 Publication of science and engineering articles by country, years 2006 and 2016 101

6.4 Percent of firms and universities willing to recommend collaborations in R&D with universities and firms in R&D, year 2017 104

6.5 United Kingdom barriers to collaboration: firm and university perspectives 105

6.6 Number of Irish underpinning intellectual property mechanisms from publicly funded research, years 2013–2019 106

6.7 List of university science parks, by country and region 108

6.8 Countries that adopted Bayh-Dole-like policies, by year of adoption 112

7.1 Major strengths of global innovation systems, by selected OECD country 118

7.2 Characteristics of the major strengths of global innovation systems, by selected OECD country 123

About the authors

James A. Cunningham is Professor of Strategic Management at Newcastle Business School, Northumbria University, Newcastle Upon Tyne, United Kingdom. He has held academic positions at University College Dublin and National University of Ireland Galway (NUI Galway). At NUI Galway he held a variety of leadership positions including Head of Strategic Management group, Executive MBA Programme Director, Director of the Centre of Innovation and Structural Change, and founding Director of the Whitaker Institute.

Professor Cunningham's research intersects the fields of strategic management, innovation, and entrepreneurship. His research focuses on strategy issues with respect to scientists as principal investigators, university technology transfer commercialization, academic, public sector and technology entrepreneurship, entrepreneurial universities, and business failure. He has papers published in leading international journals such as *Research Policy*, *Small Business Economics*, *R&D Management*, *Long Range Planning*, *Journal of Small Business Management*, *Journal of Technology Transfer*, *Technological Forecasting and Social Change*, *International Marketing Management*, and the *Journal of Rural Studies* among others. Awards for his research include six best paper conference awards and two case study international competition awards. Cunningham has published several books on the themes of strategy, entrepreneurship, technology transfer, and technology entrepreneurship with leading publishers such as Oxford University Press, Palgrave Macmillan, Routledge, Springer, and World Scientific Publishing.

Cunningham has successfully secured research funding and is an experienced principal investigator leading large-scale multi-partner publicly funded research programs for funded agencies such as Northern Peripheries Programme (European Union), the Irish Higher Education Authority, Irish Research Council, and Science Foundation Ireland; and he is regularly invited to participate in external research funding peer review panels for public funding bodies and university research programs. He is the author of numerous commissioned research reports for organizations such as the European Union Commission, Australian Skills Council, the American Chamber of Commerce, Ireland, Galway City and County Councils, Galway Chamber of Commerce, and the Creative Edge. In addition, he has contributed to policy development processes on technology transfer, innovation, and entrepreneurship in Ireland.

In 2015, he was invited by the Joint Committee on Jobs, Enterprise, and Innovation of the Irish Parliament to provide expert evidence on how to grow and develop the Irish creative economy and industries.

Cunningham regularly delivers invited keynote talks and presentations nationally and internationally to business, policy, and academic audiences as well as executive master classes on strategy development, innovation and technology entrepreneurship.

Albert N. Link is the Virginia Batte Phillips Distinguished Professor at the University of North Carolina at Greensboro (UNCG). He received the B.S. degree in mathematics from the University of Richmond (Phi Beta Kappa) and the Ph.D. degree in economics from Tulane University. After receiving the Ph.D., he joined the economics faculty at Auburn University, was later Scholar-in-Residence at Syracuse University, and then he joined the economics faculty at UNCG in 1982. In 2019, Link was awarded the title and honorary position of Visiting Professor at Northumbria University, United Kingdom.

Professor Link's research focuses on technology and innovation policy, the economics of R&D, and policy/program evaluation. He is currently the Editor-in-Chief of the *Journal of Technology Transfer*. He is also co-editor of *Foundations and Trends in Entrepreneurship* and founder/editor of *Annals of Science and Technology Policy*.

Among his more than 65 books, some of the more recent ones are: *Invention, Innovation and U.S. Federal Laboratories* (Edward Elgar, 2020), *Technology Transfer and U.S. Public Sector Innovation* (Edward Elgar, 2020), *Collaborative Research in the United States: Policies and Institutions for Cooperation among Firms* (Routledge, 2020), *Sources of Knowledge and Entrepreneurial Behavior* (University of Toronto Press, 2019), *Handbook for University Technology Transfer* (University of Chicago Press, 2015), *Public Sector Entrepreneurship: U.S. Technology and Innovation Policy* (Oxford University Press, 2015), *Bending the Arc of Innovation: Public Support of R&D in Small, Entrepreneurial Firms* (Palgrave Macmillan, 2013), *Valuing an Entrepreneurial Enterprise* (Oxford University Press, 2012), *Public Goods, Public Gains: Calculating the Social Benefits of Public R&D* (Oxford University Press, 2011), *Employment Growth from Public Support of Innovation in Small Firms* (W.E. Upjohn Institute for Employment Research, 2011), and *Government as Entrepreneur* (Oxford University Press, 2009).

Link's other research endeavors consist of more than 200 peer-reviewed journal articles and book chapters, as well as numerous government reports. His scholarship has appeared in such journals as the *American Economic Review*, the *Journal of Political Economy*, the *Review of Economics and Statistics*, *Economica*, *Research Policy*, *Economics of Innovation and New Technology*, the *European Economic Review*, *Small Business Economics*,

ISSUES in Science and Technology, *Scientometrics*, and the *Journal of Technology Transfer*.

Link's public service includes being a member of the National Research Council's research team that conducted the 2010 evaluation of the U.S. Small Business Innovation Research (SBIR) program. Based on that assignment, he testified before the U.S. Congress in April 2011 on the economic benefits associated with the SBIR program. Link also served from 2007 to 2012 as a U.S. Representative to the United Nations (in Geneva) in the capacity of co-vice chairperson of the Team of Specialists on Innovation and Competitiveness Policies Initiative for the Economic Commission for Europe. In October 2018, Link delivered the European Commission Distinguished Scholar Lecture at the European Commission's Joint Research Centre (in Seville).

Acknowledgements

First, we thank our wives, Sammi and Carol, for their patience as we progressed through the writing of this book. We also thank our colleagues at the Northumbria University and the University of North Carolina at Greensboro for their many comments and suggestions on material that formed the basis of this book.

Abbreviations

AUTM	Association of University Technology Managers
DHS	Department of Homeland Security
DOC	Department of Commerce
DOD	Department of Defense
DOE	Department of Energy
DOI	Department of Interior
DOT	Department of Transportation
EC	European Commission
ED	Department of Education
EPA	Environmental Protection Agency
EPO	European Patent Office
ERDF	European Regional Development Fund
ERTA	Economic Recovery Tax Act
EU	European Union
EU-15	European Union 15 member countries prior to 2004
FDI	foreign direct investment
G7	Group of Seven countries
GDP	Gross Domestic Product
GTIPA	Global Trade and Innovation Policy Alliance
HEIs	higher education institutions
HHS	Health and Human Services
ICT	information and communication technology
IP	intellectual property
KTPs	Knowledge Transfer Partnerships
M	millions
MFP	multi-factor productivity
MNCs	multinational corporations

NASA	National Aeronautics and Space Administration
NCRA	National Cooperative Research Act
NIH	National Institutes of Health
NIST	National Institute of Standards and Technology
NRC	National Research Council
NRC	Nuclear Regulatory Commission
NSF	National Science Foundation
OECD	Organisation for Economic Co-operation and Development
PCP	precommercial procurement program
PctR&D	percent of Gross Domestic R&D financed by the private sector
PI	principal investigator
PPP	purchasing power parity
PROs	private research organizations
R&D	research and development
R&D	research and development
R&E	research and experimentation
R&I	research and innovation
S&E	scientific and engineering
SBIR	Small Business Innovation Research
SBRI	Small Business Research Initiative
SMEs	small and medium sized enterprises
STTR	Small Business Technology Transfer
TPO	Technology Partnerships Office
TTO	technology transfer office
U.K.	United Kingdom
UKRI	UK Research and Innovation
UNESCO	United Nations Educational, Scientific and Cultural Organization
U.S.	United States
USDA	U.S. Department of Agriculture
USDOJ	U.S. Department of Justice
USPTO	U.S. Patent and Trademark Office

1. Technology and innovation policy: setting the stage

KEY TERMS: IT DEPENDS TO WHOM YOU TALK

As the title suggests, this book is about technology policy and innovation policy. We will discuss throughout this book that these two areas of policy emphasis are related and that they deserve to be presented separately as well as relatedly because the focus of each policy area is distinct. The difference between the focus of technology policy and innovation policy can simply be illustrated through definitions of the terms *technology* and *innovation*.

We emphasize the difference between the definitions of the terms *technology* and *innovation* in this introductory chapter because many policy makers, as reflected through their own statements and organizational reports as noted below, frequently subsume technology policy (often without mentioning it by name) under the rubric of innovation policy. This agglomeration may in fact be a valid supposition for a successful technology policy, but not all technology policies fulfill their purposes. Also, we think this agglomeration of technology policy under the rubric of innovation policy masks not only many subtle differences between what a technology is and what an innovation is, but also it masks important differences between the purposes of a technology policy and the purposes of an innovation policy as well as the time element between the two. In addition to policy makers, many academics have also looked at technology policy and innovation policy, with technology policy similarly subsumed under innovation policy, through the lens of national innovation systems, triple/quadruple helix frameworks, and innovation/entrepreneurial ecosystems.

We present definitions of the two terms *technology* and *innovation*, as well as other key terms, in this chapter as a starting point for the topics discussed in the chapters that follow. As we illustrate below, there is not a uniform definition of the key terms relevant to the topics presented in this book. This is the case within the academic literature as well as within the policy literature, although the definitions that are presented with reference to these literatures are generally similar.[1] We devote space here, at the beginning of this book, to several key terms not only for clarity purposes but also to emphasize the lens through which we view technology policy and innovation policy. Our point of emphasis is that technology policy and innovation policy refer to different stages in the so-called process of *lab to market*, to borrow a phrase from the topical policy vernacular.

Our starting point is to define four fundamental terms: *science*, *technology*, *innovation*, and *policy*. Our working definitions of these key terms are as follows:

- *Science*—the search for new knowledge; the search is based on observed facts and truths; science begins with known starting conditions and searches for unknown end results.
- *Technology*—the application of new knowledge, learned through science, to some practical problem.
- *Innovation*—technology put into use or commercialized.
- *Policy*—a course of action adopted and pursued by an organization, and herein the organization is assumed to be in the public sector and it is referred to generically as the government.

In our view, what follows from these four definitions is that the term *technology policy* refers to policy to enhance the application of new knowledge, which often occurs within a research and development (R&D) *laboratory* (our emphasis), and the term *innovation policy* refers to policy to enhance the commercialization of a resulting technology (if there is one), and that commercialization occurs in the *market* (our emphasis). Thus, our emphasis is on the use of the phrase *lab to market*. More formally, the terms of relevance are:

- *Technology policy*—policy to enhance, in a laboratory, the application of new knowledge, learned through science, to some known problem (science is the search for new knowledge; the search is based on observed facts and truths; science begins with known starting conditions and searches for unknown end results).[2]
- *Innovation policy*—policy to enhance the commercialization of a technology in the market.

The above definitions are collectively presented in Table 1.1 for ease of comparison and reference.

Table 1.1 *Definitions of key terms*

Key Term	Definition
Science	The search for new knowledge; the search is based on observed facts and truths; science begins with known starting conditions and searches for unknown end results.
Technology	The application of new knowledge, learned through science, to some practical problem.
Innovation	Technology put into use or commercialized.
Policy	A course of action adopted and pursued by an organization, and herein the organization is assumed to be in the public sector and it is referred to generically as the government.
Technology policy	A policy to enhance, in a laboratory, the application of new knowledge, learned through science, to some known problem (science is the search for new knowledge; the search is based on observed facts and truths; science begins with known starting conditions and searches for unknown end results).
Innovation policy	A policy to enhance the commercialization of a technology in the market.

Source: Prepared by the authors.

We are certainly not the first researchers to offer definitions of the terms *technology* and *technology policy* or of the terms *innovation* and *innovation policy*, either with respect to the activities and policy actions of one country's firms or government or of the firms and governments in a comparative group of countries. However, as we point out below, there are a number of notable policy documents that proport to advance global innovation policies; however, these documents collectively subsume the concepts of technology and technology policy within the discussion of an innovation and an innovation policy, although some of these documents even fail to define what is meant by the term *innovation.*[3]

Examples of notable policy documents in which the term *innovation* has been defined include the Global Trade and Innovation Policy Alliance's *National Innovation Policies: What Countries Do Best and How They Can Improve.* Therein it is written that (GTIPA, 2019, p. 2):[4]

> … innovation is the improvement of existing, or the creation of entirely new, products, processes, services, and business or organizational models. Put simply, innovation is about the creation of new value for the world.

And it follows from this definition of an innovation that an innovation policy is a governmental effort aimed at the improvement of existing—or the creation of entirely new—products, processes, services, and business or organizational models.

In a Nesta report, prepared by Stanley, Glennie, and Gabriel, *How Inclusive Is Innovation Policy? Insights from an International Comparison*, the following is written about innovation (Nesta, 2008, p. 6, emphasis in original):

> [W]e define innovation broadly as new ideas that are put into practice and create some kind of value … then innovation policy can be characterized *as all combined actions that are undertaken by public organizations that influence the innovation process.*

The Organisation for Economic Co-operation and Development (OECD), in its report *OECD Innovation Strategy 2015: An Agenda for Policy Action*, writes (OECD, 2015a, p. 2):

> [Innovation] involves the creation and diffusion of new products, processes and methods.

The OECD also uses this same definition in its report *The Innovation Imperative Contributing to Productivity, Growth and Well-Being* (OECD, 2015b). Elsewhere, the OECD offers, for data collection purposes, a more complete definition of the term *innovation.* According to the OECD report *The Measurement of Scientific, Technological and Innovation Activities: Oslo Manual 2018 GUIDELINES FOR COLLECTING, REPORTING AND USING DATA ON INNOVATION* (OECD, 2018b, p. 20):

> An innovation is a new or improved product or process (or combination thereof) that differs significantly from the unit's previous products or processes and that has been made available to potential users (product) or brought into use by the unit (process).

The European Commission (EC, 2020) interprets the term *innovation* in the following way:

> … to accelerate the modernization of the EU industry, the update of products and service innovation, use of innovative manufacturing technologies and the introduction of new business models is necessary. The [European] Commission develops policies that help speed up the broad commercialisation of innovation and engages in many activities that support innovation in the EU [European Union].

Innovation policy within the EU has been enshrined into law through the Treaty on the Functioning of the European Union Article 173.[5] Therein it is stated that:

> The Union and the Member States shall ensure that the conditions necessary for the competitiveness of the Union's industry exist.
>
> 1. For that purpose, in accordance with a system of open and competitive markets, their action shall be aimed at:

- speeding up the adjustment of industry to structural changes,
- encouraging an environment favourable to initiatives and to the development of undertakings throughout the Union, particularly small and medium-sized undertakings,
- encouraging an environment favourable to cooperation between undertakings,
- fostering better exploitation of the industrial potential of policies of innovation, research and technological development.

2. The Member States shall consult each other in liaison with the Commission and, where necessary, shall coordinate their action. The Commission may take any useful initiative to promote such coordination, in particular initiatives aiming at the establishment of guidelines and indicators, the organisation of exchange of best practice, and the preparation of the necessary elements for periodic monitoring and evaluation. The European Parliament shall be kept fully informed.
3. The Union shall contribute to the achievement of the objectives set out in paragraph 1 through the policies and activities it pursues under other provisions of the Treaties. The European Parliament and the Council, acting in accordance with the ordinary legislative procedure and after consulting the Economic and Social Committee, may decide on specific measures in support of action taken in the Member States to achieve the objectives set out in paragraph 1, excluding any harmonisation of the laws and regulations of the Member States.

The *European Innovation Scorecard* and *Regional Innovation Scorecard* are both mechanisms that are used to evaluate innovation policy performance across Member States in the EU. The EU Framework Programmes, European Regional Development Fund (ERDF), and different financial instruments are policy approaches that the EU has used to implement innovation policy across the Member States. For example, the current EU Framework Programme, Horizon Europe 2021 to 2027, further affirms the continued objective "to support the whole R&I [research and innovation] cycle in an integrated manner."[6]

With respect to research and technology development, the Treaty on the Function of the European Union devotes Articles 179 to 190 to outlining the legal basis of the EU's approach in this regard. Article 179 states;

1. The Union shall have the objective so strengthening its scientific and technological bases by achieving a European research area in which researchers, scientific knowledge and technology circulate freely, and encouraging it to become more competitive, including in its industry, while promoting all the research activities deemed necessary by virtue of other Chapters of Treaties.
2. For this purpose the Union shall, throughout the Union, encourage undertakings, including small and medium-sized undertakings, research centres and universities in their research and technological development activities of high quality; it shall support their efforts to cooperate with one another, aiming, notably, at permitting researchers to cooperate freely across borders and at enabling undertakings to exploit the internal market potential to the full, in particular through

the opening-up of national public contracts, the definition of common standards the removal of legal and fiscal obstacles to that cooperation.

3. All Union activities under the Treaties in the area of research and technological development including demonstration projects, shall be decided on and implemented in accordance with the provisions of this Title.

Article 180 of the Treaty on the Function of the European Union emphasizes complementary activities across Member States in the development of research progress:

> In pursuing these objectives, the Union shall carry out the following activities, complementing the activities carried out in the Member States:
>
> (a) implementation of research, technological development and demonstration programmes, by promoting cooperation with and between undertakings, research centres and universities;
>
> (b) promotion of cooperation in the field of Union research, technological development and demonstration with third world countries and international organisations;
>
> (c) dissemination and optimization of the results of activities in Union research, technological development and demonstration;
>
> (d) stimulation of the training and mobility of researchers in the Union.

These two articles, Article 179 and Article 180, in the Treaty on the Function of the European Union provide the legal basis that has led to the creation of the European Framework Programmes, the European Research Area Net (created in 2002), and the European Institute of Innovation Technology (created in 2008).

With these definitions and/or key terms in mind, and we emphasize again that technology and technology policy are not explicit building blocks for innovation and innovation policy in the text of the sample of definitions from the policy reports quoted above, a logical more general question to ask is: Why is technology policy important, and: Why is innovation policy important?

Our response to these two questions is not independent from how we approach the actions that fall under the rubrics of technology policy and innovation policy; that is, our response to these two questions reflects the lens through which we wrote this book.

One might choose to study technology policy and innovation policy in somewhat structured terms. Such an approach to the study of technology policy and innovation policy might take the following contextual form. One would learn under this structure that policy A was adopted in year x for the purpose of …; policy B was adopted in year y for the purpose of … . The importance of studying technology policy and innovation policy in this manner is to characterize the context in which economic growth (discussed below) occurs.

However, if one chooses to study technology policy and innovation policy from an assessment or evaluation perspective, one might learn to associate policy A with a unique performance dimension associated with economic growth, and to associate policy B with another performance dimension associated with economic growth. Thus, a comparison of the impact of policy A with policy B necessitates metrics to quantify dimensions of economic growth (see Link, 1993, 2006).

Many studies have demonstrated that technology policy does have an impact on economic performance and thus on economic growth (see Dasgupta and Stoneman, 2005; Metcalfe, 1994). Technology policy also has an impact on the performance of firms (see Zahra and Covin, 1993). More recently, a vein in the academic literature has begun to explore the societal impacts of technology policy by researchers from a number of different disciplines (see Fini et al., 2018; Fisher, 2005; Schillo and Kinder, 2017).

In designing such technology policies, Mowery (1983), as an example, argued the need for policy makers to focus on both the supply of research and development (R&D) and its allocation among participants during the technology development process. Similarly, studies have also examined the impact of innovation policy at an economic level (see Asheim, 2019; Fagerberg, 2017; Flanagan et al., 2011; Kuhlmann, 2001; Mazzucato, 2017), at a firm level (see Becker, 2019; Tang et al., 2018; Wadho and Chaudhry, 2018), and at the level of society as a whole (see Esmaeilpoorarabi et al., 2018; Mazzucato et al., 2020).

Moreover, the evolution to innovation policy in some countries has emanated from industrial policy (see Cunningham et al., 2020; Soete, 2007), and this perspective is set against a changing conceptualization of innovation (see Meissner et al., 2017). Researchers have argued, and have supported their arguments with references to empirical studies in the academic literature, that the importance of innovation policy is related to how it focuses on and considers issues such as societal grand challenges (see Coenen et al., 2015; Hayter and Link, 2020), sectoral challenges (see Hall, 2009), as well as the support and enhancement of regional innovation (see Cunningham et al., 2019a).

Over the previous decades, researchers have attempted to conceptualize and evaluate empirically the relationship between technology policies and innovation policies, and the affected parties of individuals, firms, and the public sector or government. Technology and innovation policies are primarily intended to support and advance economic growth that might then result in second order impacts that have net benefits for society and its citizens. Such a conceptualization (see Piazza and Abrahamson, 2020) has evolved considerably over time in part to deal with complex and nuanced policy challenges that policy makers face when crafting and implementing effective technology policies and innovation policies that result in a tangible, if not a transformative, change for end users or recipients of such policies. This evolution has also been driven by a number of significant and accelerated changes across different industrial sectors brought about by technological advancements, more effective firm-level knowledge management practices, and firm-level business models of innovation per se and of the management of innovation (see Birkinshaw et al., 2008; Chesbrough, 2010; Darroch, 2005). Such conceptualizations have been formulated on the basis of national innovation systems (see Cunningham and Golden, 2015; Freeman, 2002; Lundvall, 2007), industrial clusters (see Feldman et al., 2005; Green et al., 2001; Iammarino and McCann, 2006), triple helix models (see Leydesdorff and Etzkowitz, 1998: Leydesdorff and Meyer, 2003), quadruple helix models (see Carayannis and Campbell, 2009; Miller et al., 2016), entrepreneurial ecosystems (see Audretsch et al., 2019a; Cantner et al., 2020; Cunningham et al., 2019b; Spigel, 2017; Spigel and Harrison, 2018), and innovation ecosystems (see Autio and Thomas, 2014; Oh et al., 2016; Walrave et al., 2018). Such conceptualizations are generally temporal in nature because the policy challenges that they are attempting to address require an approach that results not only in the advancement of knowledge, but also in a message that is appealing and relevant to policy makers and their constituents.

This book contains elements of many previous approaches to the study of technology policy and innovation policy. We emphasize in this book, where appropriate, the context in which a technology policy or an innovation policy is promulgated. We also emphasize, where appropriate, assessment and evaluation perspectives related to a technology policy or an innovation policy.[7]

THE IMPORTANCE OF INNOVATION POLICY

Staying within the context of the policy references quoted just above, and keeping in mind that these policy references implicitly as well as explicitly subsume technology policy under the rubric of innovation policy (although that pedagogical masking was not explicitly stated within the context of the quoted phrases above), we note in this section of this chapter the economic growth implications that are attributable to innovation policies.

The Global Trade and Innovation Policy Alliance, in its *National Innovation Policies: What Countries Do Best and How They Can Improve*, wrote (GTIPA, 2019, p. 2):

> Innovation matters because it's the foundational source of long-term global economic growth and improvements in quality of life and standards of living.

The OECD wrote in *The Innovation Imperative Contributing to Productivity, Growth and Well-Being* (2015b, p. 17):

> A key interest of policy makers in innovation has long been around its potential contribution to economic growth.

Finally, the U.S. National Research Council (NRC) wrote in its report *Capturing Change in Science, Technology, and Innovation: Improving Indicators to Inform Policy* (NRC, 2014, p. 44):

> … it is clear that as a national goal, policies that encourage bringing more innovations to market are useful if they generate economic growth and jobs and improve the nation's competitiveness.

Our approach to presenting an international perspective on technology policy and innovation policy is guided in part by (or should we say, limited in part by) our experiences and relative familiarity with U.K. and U.S. technology policy and innovation policy. Accordingly, we ask: What was the genesis of emphasis on innovation policy which led to the association between innovation and economic growth? And our contemporary answer relates to the productivity slowdown that was pervasive in most industrialized nations beginning in the early 1970s.

Our empirical illustrations related to technology policy and innovation policy focus in detail on the U.K. and the U.S. experiences, and to a lesser extent on the experiences of other international countries for which data are available. Of course, policies in all countries merit an in-depth study. In fact, a number of detailed descriptive studies of innovation policies across OECD member companies have been prepared. Looking ahead, in Chapter 7 we will offer generalizations from these OECD studies as an effort toward a more encompassing and comprehensive international study of national innovation policies.[8]

THE PRODUCTIVITY SLOWDOWN: AN INTERNATIONAL GLIMPSE

From an international perspective, Figures 1.1, 1.2, and 1.3 show the annual percentage change in Gross Domestic Product (GDP) per capita, in constant prices, in the United Kingdom, the United States, and the G7 countries (Canada, France, Germany, Italy, Japan, the United Kingdom, and the United States).[9] This index, GDP per capita, measures a dimension of labor productivity over the years 1971 through 2019.[10] Ideally, we would like to have illustrated total factor productivity (also referred to as multi-factor productivity) over time, but the OECD data on that index began only in 1985 (a few years after the productivity slowdown, discussed below, had ended).[11]

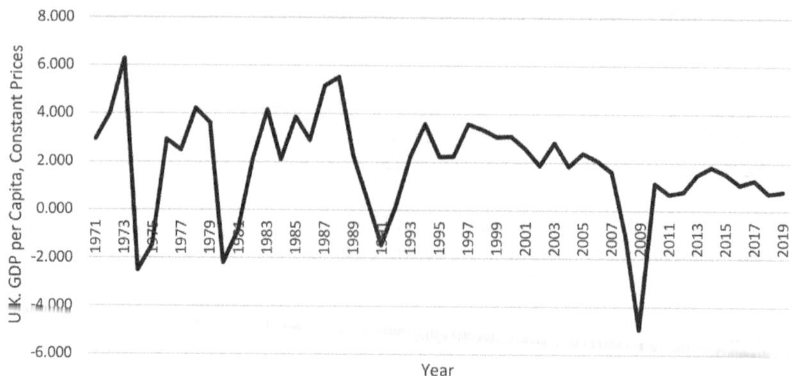

Source: https://stats.oecd.org/Index.aspx?DataSetCode=MSTI_PUB (accessed September 16, 2020).

Figure 1.1 *Annual percentage change in U.K. Gross Domestic Product per capita in constant prices*

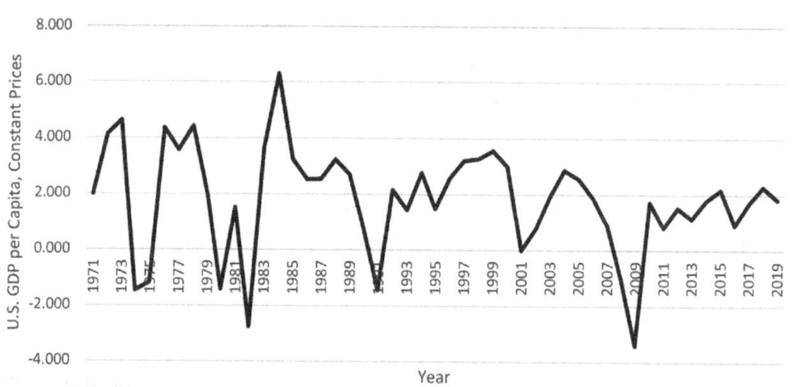

Source: https://stats.oecd.org/Index.aspx?DataSetCode=MSTI_PUB (accessed September 16, 2020).

Figure 1.2 *Annual percentage change in U.S. Gross Domestic Product per capita in constant prices*

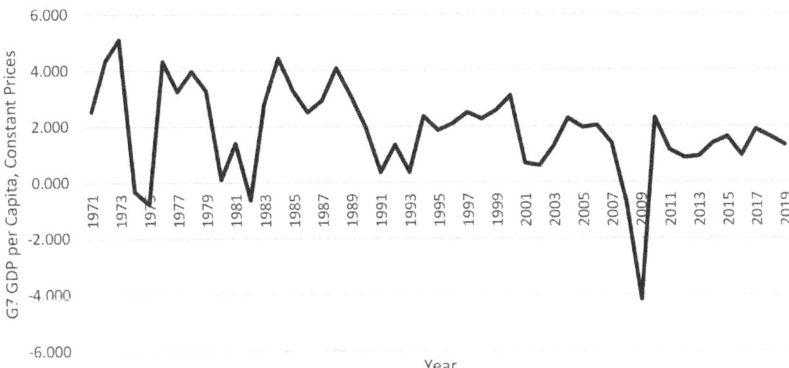

Source: https://stats.oecd.org/Index.aspx?DataSetCode=MSTI_PUB (accessed September 16, 2020).

Figure 1.3 *Annual percentage change in G7 Gross Domestic Product per capita in constant prices*

In the United Kingdom, the United States, and the G7 countries as a group, measured labor productivity declined in the early 1970s and then again in the late 1970s and early 1980s. In fact, the labor productivity declines during these periods are rivaled in the post-World War II period only by the Great Recession of 2007–2009.

Many argue that the initial decline in labor productivity (and multi-factor productivity) was associated with the 1973 oil crisis and the production method adjustments by industry that followed. The subsequent declines have been associated, often in a causal manner, with a decline in investments in R&D, and investments in R&D have long been associated with new technologies being developed and then entering the market. Thus, the relevant literatures have focused on variations of the following paradigm:

R&D → technology → innovation → economic growth

This paradigm has often been referred to as the linear model, and it is generally referenced to Bush's *Science—the Endless Frontier* (1945), more in terms of conceptualization than explicitly by name.[12] The *innovation → economic growth* portion of this paradigm is perhaps what underlies the arguments posed above about the consequence of innovation policy. However, to the extent that this paradigm has construct validity, it buttresses our argument that the innovation flows from new technology and thus effective technology policy, focused on R&D investments, is a relevant prerequisite to consider for the development of innovation policy.

A ROADMAP OF THE CHAPTERS THAT FOLLOW

In Chapter 2, we focus on technology policies to enhance private-sector R&D. We first describe private-sector R&D investments across countries and over time. Then, we ask why a country needs a technology policy to enhance its private-sector's investments in R&D, and we answer that question in terms of the economics concept of market failure. We focus on both direct and indirect incentives by the government to encourage firms to investment more in R&D.

Chapter 2 segues to Chapter 3 in which we discuss, in an exploratory manner, the effectiveness of technology policies to enhance private-sector R&D. In Chapter 3 we offer some descriptive empirical insight into the effectiveness of the two technology policies discussed in Chapter 2: tax incentives and direct subsidies. We also introduce a framework for explaining the role of investments in R&D and the role of technology policy and innovation policy in the economy as well as the relationship between the two policies.

In Chapter 4, we continue to explore dimensions of the effectiveness of U.S. direct subsidies to R&D.

In Chapter 5, we discuss the technology policy environment in which private-sector investments in R&D occur. Key infrastructural elements of that environment are a country's patent system and incentives in place to encourage R&D collaborations.

In Chapter 6, we discuss technology policies to leverage public-sector R&D. The policies that we discuss focus on incentives aimed at the public sector's efforts to encourage knowledge transfers from universities and national laboratories to the private sector.

Chapter 7 summarizes key findings from OECD reports on the innovation policies in various countries in an effort to identify common characteristics, and thus to give construct validity to the framework that we developed in the earlier chapters.

Finally, in Chapter 8, we offer concluding observations about technology and innovation policies across countries. We also include in this chapter a discussion of a technology policy ecosystem in which actors play a critical role in the development and implementation of technology policies reflected in the technology policy environment.

NOTES

1. As Audretsch et al. (2019b, p. 2) point out, different academic disciplines view the concept of innovation differently. These authors offered the following generalizations. In the field of finance, innovation is viewed in terms of the "allocation by firms of financial resources to innovative activities and the accessing by those firms of funds to finance innovation." In the field of entrepreneurship, innovation is characterized as follows: "Innovation-driven firms and entrepreneurs engage with a variety of knowledge providers (collaborations, spillovers) while also investing in research and development to disrupt the market equilibrium by introducing new ideas, products and services." In the field of management, innovation is viewed in terms of the "access and development of the capacity, skills and resources to identify, pursue and coordinate innovation in processes, products, management and business models." Finally, in the area of marketing, innovation captures the "creation of a steady stream of new products and services that meets the needs of customers." We add to these alternative conceptualizations the economics view that an innovation is defined in terms of a shift in a production function.
2. Our use of the phrase *in a laboratory* is not intended to dismiss entrepreneurial actions that lead to a new technology. For some entrepreneurs, the appropriate *laboratory* might be a basement or garage. That said, the technology policies that we discuss in this book are generally aimed at institutions performing R&D. Accordingly, levels of investments in R&D are in general the target variable for technology policy.
3. Many researchers point to Schumpeter for a foundational definition of an innovation, but as Hébert and Link (2009) point out, the notion of an innovation traces to scholars much before the time of Schumpeter's writings. That said, it is important to acknowledge Schumpeter's view of innovation because his is the view that arguably is most closely related to entrepreneurial behavior in the modern literature. What follows in the rest of this note is paraphrased text directly from Hébert and Link (2009).

   Schumpeter described innovation in terms of new combinations that underlie economic development. These combinations included the following: (1) creation of a new good or new quality of good; (2) creation of a new method of production; (3) the opening of a new market; (4) the capture of a new source of supply; (5) a new organization of industry (e.g., creation or destruction of a monopoly). Over time, these new combinations dissipate, as the new becomes part of the old (i.e., a circular flow). But, this evolution does not change the essence of the entrepreneurial function.

   More specifically, Schumpeter defined innovation with reference to a production function, which (Schumpeter, 1939, p. 62) "describes the way in which quantity of product varies if quantities of factors vary. If, instead of quantities of factors, we vary the form of the function, we have an innovation." Note our conceptualization of the economics view of innovation in note 1 above. Regarding the source of innovation, Schumpeter recognized that the knowledge that kindles an innovation need not be new (Schumpeter, 1928, p. 378): "it is not the knowledge that matters, but the successful solution of the task *sui generis* of putting an untried method into practice—there may be, and often is, no scientific novelty involved at all, and even if it be involved, this does not make any difference to the nature of the process."

In Schumpeter's theory, successful innovation depends, therefore, on leadership, not intelligence, and it should not be confused with invention. The leadership that constitutes innovation in the Schumpeterian system is not homogeneous. According to Schumpeter (1928, p. 380), different aptitudes for the routine work of "static" management result merely in differential success at what all managers do, whereas different leadership aptitudes mean that "some are able to undertake uncertainties incident to what has not been done before; [indeed] … to overcome these difficulties incident to change of practice is the function of the entrepreneur."

4. The Global Trade and Innovation Policy Alliance (GTIPA, 2019, p. 1) "is a global network of independent think tanks that are ardent supporters of greater global trade liberalization and integration, deplore trade-distorting 'innovation mercantilist' practices, but yet believe that governments can and should play important and proactive roles in spurring greater innovation and productivity in their enterprises and economies. Member organizations advocate and adhere to research and policy consistent with a core Statement of Shared Principles."
5. See Official Journal of the European Union, Consolidated Version of the Treaty on the Functioning of the European Union at: https://eur-lex.europa.eu/LexUriServ/LexUriServ.do?uri=CELEX:12012E/TXT:EN:PDF (accessed September 15, 2020).
6. See European Commission (EC, 2018) *Proposal for a Regulation of the European Parliament and of the Council Establishing Horizon Europe—the Framework Programme for Research and Innovation*. Therein, the EC sets forth its rules for participation and dissemination. See https://www.europarl.europa.eu/RegData/docs_autres_institutions/commission_europeenne/com/2018/0435/COM_COM(2018)0435_EN.pdf (accessed September 15, 2020).
7. As Link and Scott (2011) explain, a policy assessment is based primarily on the criterion of effectiveness: Has a policy met its stated goals and objectives? Have its designated outputs been achieved? A policy evaluation is based on the criterion of efficiency: How do the social benefits or outcomes associated with the policy compare to the social costs?
8. See https://www.oecd.org/sti/inno/oecd-reviews-of-innovation-policy.htm (accessed September 16, 2020).
9. The so-called Group of Seven (G7) countries are among the largest and wealthiest countries in the world.
10. We will rely throughout this book on international data primarily from the OECD. The years of available data will vary across the metrics that we consider. In all cases, we will use an appropriate number of years of information to illustrate our policy points.
11. A total factor productivity or multi-factor productivity index is the preferable metric through which to measure aggregate productivity trends at the national level. When available, even for a limited number of years, we will consider multi-factor productivity indices. A primer on the construction of a multi-factor productivity index is at: https://www.bls.gov/mfp/mprtech.htm (accessed September 16, 2020).
12. An excellent discussion of the linear model concept is in Godin (2006).

2. Technology policies to enhance private-sector R&D

INTRODUCTION

In this chapter, we discuss cross-country trends in private-sector investments in R&D in various countries, and we correlate those investments with performance dimensions of economic growth. A descriptive statistical analysis, especially an exploratory one, might initially appear to be off topic given the step-by-step approach to the policy paradigm that we suggested in Chapter 1, namely:

R&D → technology → innovation → economic growth

However, from our perspective it is definitely not. Our purpose in showing a relationship of the form *R&D → economic growth* in Chapter 1 was to emphasize the importance of private-sector investments in R&D as a, if not the, relevant target variable of technology policy for bringing about a new technology, which will then stimulate economic growth in an industrialized country as it is put to use as an innovation (Link and Cunningham, 2021). That said, in subsequent chapters we will also discuss the impact of public-sector investments in R&D on economic growth as well as the complementary nature of private-sector and public-sector investments in R&D.

Along with our emphasis in this chapter on private-sector investments in R&D as the target variable for technology policy comes a related policy question: Is the private sector investing in R&D at a socially optimal level? And, if the answer to this question is "No," then the relevant follow-on question becomes: What technology policies will be needed to increase the level of private-sector investments in R&D from its current level to a socially optimal level?

As governments pursue technology policies, complemented by entrepreneurship and innovation policies designed to stimulate sustainable economic growth across sectoral settings and regions, the fundamental policy issue that we raise, and that Bilbao-Osorio and Rodríguez-Pose (2004) and others have also raised, is whether these policies are paying off.

PRIVATE-SECTOR INVESTMENTS IN R&D

Significant research attention has been given to private-sector investments in R&D, and it has focused on different policies in various country settings (see Becker, 2015; Kim, 2000; Naseem et al., 2010; Wang et al., 2018). Some of this research by these and other scholars has highlighted that such private-sector investments in R&D have a greater economic impact on economic growth than public-sector investments in R&D; one such example is the case of information and communication technology (ICT) R&D investments in Korea (see Hong, 2017).

A natural strategic consideration for private-sector firms that invest in R&D is the return they earn or expect to earn on their investments in R&D as well as the mitigation of any internal organizational risks. Related to this private-sector firm consideration is a public-sector consideration. Policy makers are concerned with evaluating policy effectiveness and how the policy mix that they have deployed stimulates and supports private-sector investments in R&D. For example, policy makers are logically concerned about whether or not a current policy mix has increased the level of private-sector investments in R&D across the economy to an appropriate level, as well as the impact of the current policy mix on firm-level productivity. At the micro level, policy makers are concerned about whether or not the current policy mix is effective in providing firm leadership teams with the confidence to decide to make and maintain substantive investments in R&D. It is important that substantive investments in R&D not only have the potential to generate an economic return, but also that they have the potential to enhance the competitive position of the firm in existing markets as well as to encourage the firm to create and pursue new market opportunities. Toward these ends, firms as well as policy makers employ different approaches and methodologies to assess the economic returns to a policy mix (see Link, 1993).

Other policy considerations relate to the complementarity of private-sector investments in R&D and public-sector investments in R&D (see David et al., 2000; Görg and Strobl, 2007), and whether or not public-sector investments in R&D are necessary to stimulate private-sector R&D investments (see González and Pazó, 2008).

For the purpose of international comparisons using international data, we are defining the private sector to be synonymous with what the OECD refers to as the business enterprise sector. Table 2.1 shows, by selected countries and by country groups, the percent of gross domestic expenditures on R&D, financed by the private sector over the years 1981 through 2017.[1] With the exception of the United Kingdom, just over 50 percent of gross domestic expenditures on R&D has been financed by the private sector over this time period.

Table 2.1 *Mean percent of gross domestic R&D financed by firms in the private sector, by country and country groups, years 1981–2017*

Country and Country Group	Mean Percent (%)
United Kingdom	47.08
United States	59.08
G7 countries	55.24
EU-15 countries	54.01
OECD countries	59.36

Source: https://www.oecd.org/sti/inno/researchanddevelopmentstatisticsrds.htm (accessed October 16, 2020).
Note: The EU-15 countries include Austria, Belgium, Denmark, Finland, France, Germany, Greece, Ireland, Italy, Luxembourg, Netherlands, Portugal, Spain, Sweden, and the United Kingdom. The list of OECD countries, by date of deposit of their instruments of ratification, is at: https://www.oecd.org/about/document/list-oecd-member-countries.htm (accessed October 17, 2020).

Our emphasis on private-sector investments in R&D in this chapter, as opposed to public-sector investments in R&D, stems from the academic literature related to the returns to R&D. That literature shows that the *direct* (our emphasis) returns to private-sector investments in R&D is large, especially when R&D is accounted for by its character of use (i.e., basic research, applied research, and development), in comparison to the returns to public-sector investments in R&D.[2]

Regarding the level of investments in R&D by private-sector firms versus the level of investments in R&D that are performed in the private sector, regardless of the country or sector in which the investments originate, consider Figures 2.1 through 2.6. Figures 2.1 and 2.2 show the comparison between the sources of investments in R&D and performance of R&D for the United Kingdom, Figures 2.3 and 2.4 show this comparison for the United States, and Figures 2.5 and 2.6 show this comparison for the G7 countries.

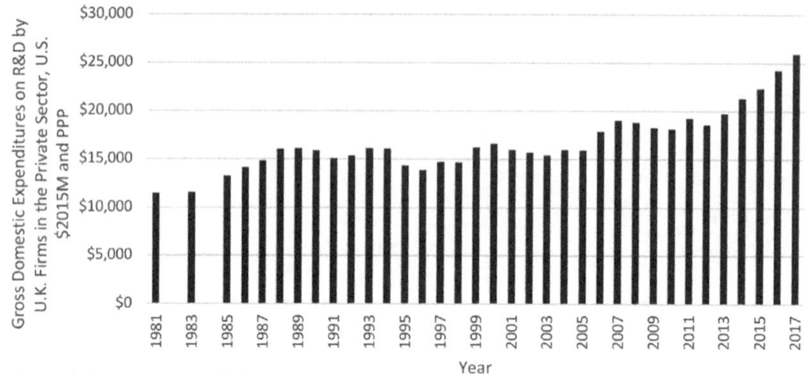

Source: https://www.oecd.org/sti/inno/researchanddevelopmentstatisticsrds.htm (accessed October 16, 2020).
Note: PPP refers to Purchasing Power Parity.

Figure 2.1 *Gross domestic expenditures on R&D by U.K. firms in the private sector, U.S. $2015M and PPP*

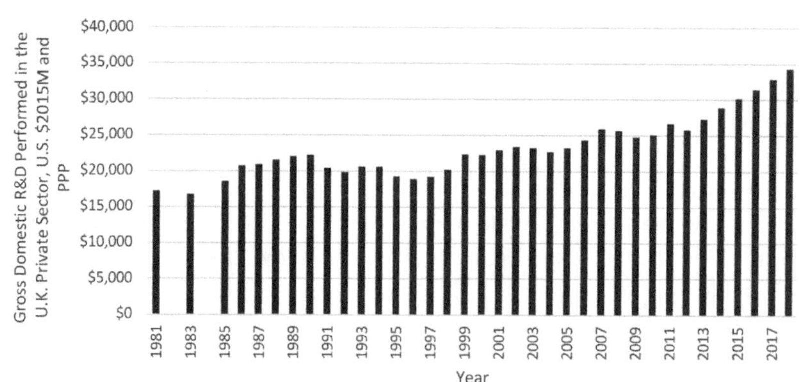

Source: https://www.oecd.org/sti/inno/researchanddevelopmentstatisticsrds.htm (accessed October 16, 2020).
Note: PPP refers to Purchasing Power Parity.

Figure 2.2 *Gross domestic R&D performed in the U.K. private sector, U.S. $2015M and PPP*

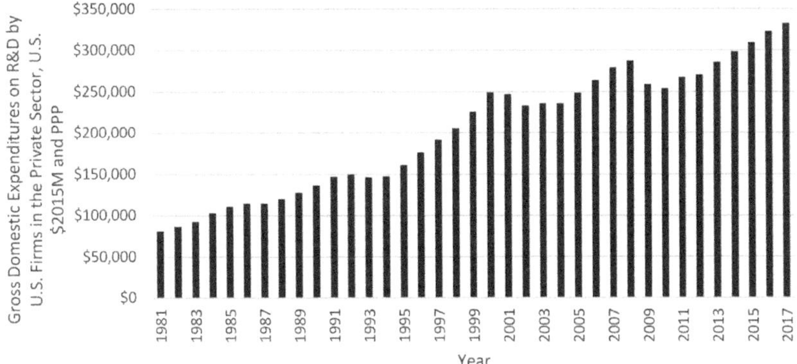

Source: https://www.oecd.org/sti/inno/researchanddevelopmentstatisticsrds.htm (accessed October 16, 2020).
Note: PPP refers to Purchasing Power Parity.

Figure 2.3 *Gross domestic expenditures on R&D by U.S. firms in the private sector, U.S. $2015M and PPP*

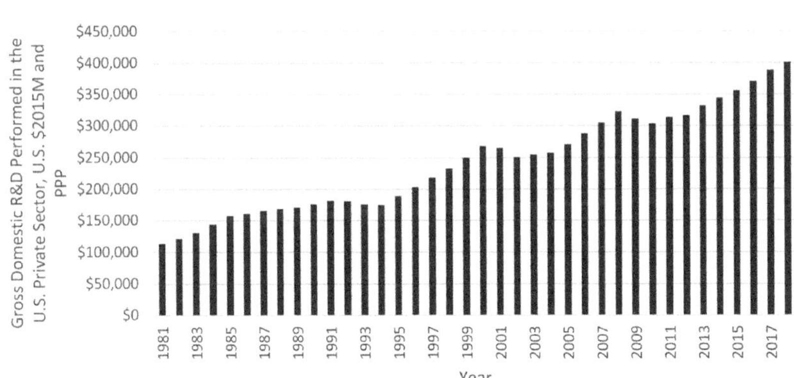

Source: https://www.oecd.org/sti/inno/researchanddevelopmentstatisticsrds.htm (accessed October 16, 2020).
Note: PPP refers to Purchasing Power Parity.

Figure 2.4 *Gross domestic R&D performed in the U.S. private sector, U.S. $2015M and PPP*

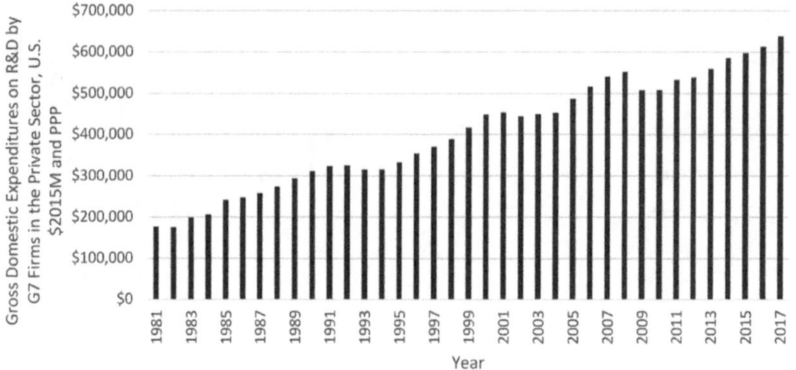

Source: https://www.oecd.org/sti/inno/researchanddevelopmentstatisticsrds.htm (accessed October 18, 2020).
Note: PPP refers to Purchasing Power Parity.

Figure 2.5 Gross domestic expenditures on R&D by G7 firms in the private sector, U.S. $2015M and PPP

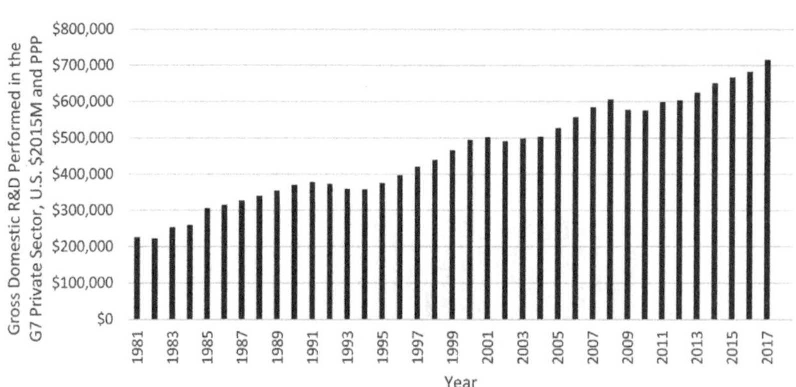

Source: https://www.oecd.org/sti/inno/researchanddevelopmentstatisticsrds.htm (accessed October 20, 2020).
Note: PPP refers to Purchasing Power Parity.

Figure 2.6 Gross domestic R&D performed in the G7 private sector, U.S. $2015M and PPP

There are at least two trends to observe from a comparison of the country's source of R&D versus performance of R&D data (i.e., Figure 2.1 compared to Figure 2.2, and so forth). First, the trend patterns in the funding of R&D by private-sector firms and the performance of R&D in the private sector, regardless of the source of the R&D, are visually similar over time. Generally, downturns in dollar amounts of both occurred during periods of economic slowdown, and upturns in dollar amounts occurred during periods of economic expansion. In fact, the correlation coefficient between the amounts of investments in R&D by private-sector firms and the amount of investments in R&D performed by firms in the private sector regardless of source, for all years of available data, ranges over the seven countries considered (i.e., each of the G7 countries) between 0.975 and 0.999. Second, over the years for which data are available, the amount of investments in R&D performed in the private sector is greater than the amount of investments in R&D financed by firms in the private sector. In other words, a portion of investments in R&D performed by firms in the private sector of a country is funded by sources outside of the private sector of that country, and most of that outside funding comes from the international sector (i.e., what is referred to in the OECD tables by the term *the rest of the world*).

From an international perspective, Table 2.2 shows the percent of total country (listed alphabetically) investments in R&D financed by firms in the private sector for year 2017. Japan and Korea are at the top of the list.

Table 2.2 *Percent of gross domestic R&D financed by firms in the private sector, by country for year 2017*

Country	Percent (%)
Australia	NA
Austria	54.65
Belgium	63.49
Canada	42.67
Chile	31.43
Czech Republic	39.32
Denmark	58.52
Estonia	43.57
Finland	58.01
France	56.08
Germany	66.18
Greece	44.77
Hungary	52.68

Country	Percent (%)
Iceland	36.42
Ireland	*48.99*
Israel	35.77
Italy	53.68
Japan	78.27
Korea	76.23
Latvia	24.15
Lithuania	35.42
Luxembourg	49.58
Mexico	19.05
Netherlands	51.63
New Zealand	46.40
Norway	42.83
Poland	52.54
Portugal	46.51
Slovak Republic	49.03
Slovenia	63.15
Spain	47.79
Sweden	60.76
Switzerland	67.04
Turkey	49.45
United Kingdom	*51.77*
United States	62.48

Source: https://www.oecd.org/sti/inno/researchanddevelopmentstatisticsrds.htm (accessed October 20, 2020).
Note: Values in italics are for year 2016.

In Table 2.3, column (1) shows the amount of private-sector investments in R&D across countries (listed alphabetically) for year 2017, and column (2) shows the amount of investments in R&D performed in the private sector across countries for year 2017. In *every* (our emphasis) country, the amount of R&D performed in the country's private sector is greater than the amount of R&D invested by firms in the country's private sector. The dollar amounts in Table 2.3, and in many of the following tables, are in terms of $2015 adjusted for purchasing power parity (PPP).

Table 2.3 *Private-sector firm investments in R&D and R&D performed in the private sector, by country for year 2017, U.S. $2015M and PPP*

Country	(1) Investments in R&D ($)	(2) Performance of R&D ($)
Australia	NA	11,201.0
Austria	7,514.6	9,607.0
Belgium	9,103.8	10,068.3
Canada	11,835.6	14,508.1
Chile	468.7	510.5
Czech Republic	2,674.9	4,275.6
Denmark	5,243.1	5,792.4
Estonia	234.1	253.5
Finland	3,909.5	4,397.9
France	34,768.9	40,462.1
Germany	82,840.4	86,490.9
Greece	1,493.4	1,626.7
Hungary	1,963.7	2,725.3
Iceland	138.1	244.0
Ireland	*1,927.7*	3,394.2
Israel	5,509.9	13,523.7
Italy	16,985.0	19,732.9
Japan	132,429.7	133,324.9
Korea	67,198.7	69,994.7
Latvia	64.5	72.6
Lithuania	284.2	295.4
Luxembourg	395.7	445.2
Mexico	1,464.7	1,729.5
Netherlands	9,175.7	10,327.8
New Zealand	1,161.1	1,381.5
Norway	2,862.8	3,516.7
Poland	5,996.7	7,361.0
Portugal	1,991.4	2,158.7
Slovak Republic	742.1	819.1
Slovenia	831.8	985.0
Spain	9,942.6	11,435.2
Sweden	10,293.0	12,083.4
Switzerland	12,381.6	12,817.2
Turkey	10,590.9	12,181.9
United Kingdom	25,952.2	32,870.4
United States	333,206.1	388,680.0

Source: https://www.oecd.org/sti/inno/researchanddevelopmentstatisticsrds.htm (accessed October 20, 2020).
Note: Values in italics are for year 2016.

PRIVATE-SECTOR INVESTMENTS IN R&D AND PRODUCTIVITY GROWTH

In this section, we suggest that private-sector investments in R&D are correlated with productivity growth measured in terms of a multi-factor productivity index. This relationship follows directly from our starting paradigm:

$$R\&D \rightarrow technology \rightarrow innovation \rightarrow economic\ growth$$

The following illustrations are specific to the United Kingdom and the United States. Figure 2.7 illustrates the annual growth in multi-factor productivity for the United Kingdom, and Figure 2.8 illustrates the annual growth in multi-factor productivity for the United States. Recessionary periods are visible from these two figures in terms of periods of negative multi-factor productivity growth.

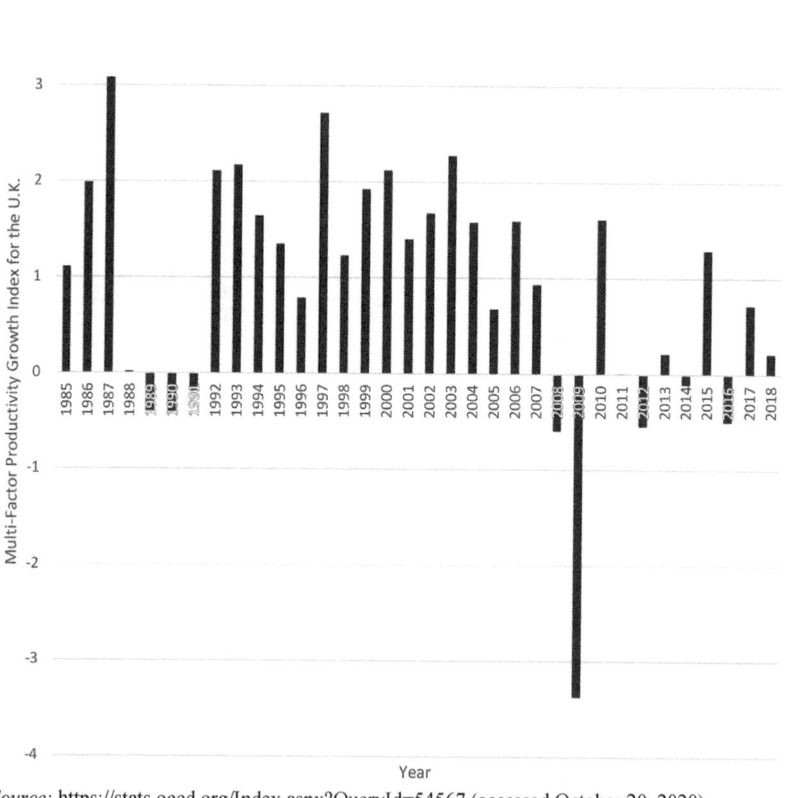

Source: https://stats.oecd.org/Index.aspx?QueryId=54567 (accessed October 20, 2020).

Figure 2.7 *Multi-factor productivity growth index for the United Kingdom, years 1985–2018*

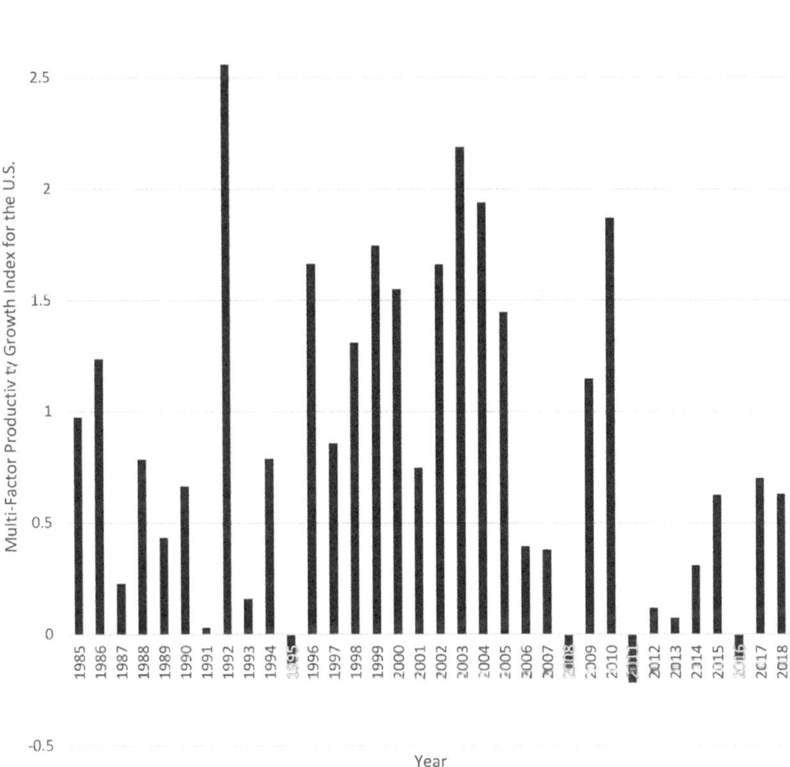

Source: https://stats.oecd.org/Index.aspx?QueryId=54567 (accessed October 20, 2020).

Figure 2.8 *Multi-factor productivity growth index for the United States, years 1985–2018*

For these two countries we considered a statistical model of the general form:

$$MFP = \mathrm{f}\,(PctR\&D,\ Recession) \tag{2.1}$$

where the variable *MFP* is the annual growth in multi-factor productivity, measured in logarithmic terms, the variable *PctR&D* is the lagged (1 year and 2 years) annual percent of gross domestic R&D financed by the private (i.e., business enterprise) sector, and the variable *Recession* controls for fixed effects during each country's recessionary periods. The data cover the period 1985 through 2018.

The 1-year lagged private-sector *PctR&D* variable is not statistically significant in either country's model, but the 2-year lagged private-sector *PctR&D* variable is. The estimated coefficients on the 2-year lagged variables are, for the two countries respectively, 0.2373 ($\rho = 0.071$) and 0.2248 ($\rho = 0.046$).[3] For the United Kingdom, these findings suggest that an increase in the percent of gross domestic R&D financed by the private sector of 10 percentage points is associated with a 2.373 percent increase in the country's multi-factor productivity growth index two years in advance; the mean of the U.K. multi-factor productivity growth index is 0.8961. For the United States, these findings suggest that an increase in the percent of gross domestic R&D financed by the private sector of 10 percentage points is associated with a 2.248 percent increase in the country's multi-factor productivity growth index two years in advance; the mean of the U.S. multi-factor productivity growth index is 0.842.

We interpret these descriptive (and exploratory) findings, for these two countries of emphasis, as suggestive evidence that private-sector investments in R&D do matter, and they matter from a policy perspective for increasing multi-factor productivity growth. Relatedly, Lichtenberg and Siegel (1991, p. 203), using U.S. data over the period 1972 through 1985, found that private-sector R&D yielded a positive economic return as well as what they termed a *productivity premium* for basic research. Other studies have found evidence of how private-sector investments in R&D contribute to firm-level productivity (see Hu, 2001; Kafouros, 2005; Lichtenberg, 1992). An early study of U.S. private-sector R&D investments among large manufacturing firms between 1957 and 1977 found that investments in R&D contributed positively to productivity growth (see Griliches, 1986). Private-sector investments in R&D can have nearly three times the impact of public-sector R&D on multi-factor productivity (see Tsai and Wang, 2004). Guellec and van Pottelsberghe de la Potterie (2001, p. 103), based on data from 16 OECD countries from 1980 through 1998, concluded that:

> ... an increase in 1 per cent in business R&D generates 0.13 per cent in productivity growth. The effect is larger in countries that are intensive in business R&D ...

As multi-factor productivity growth increases, so does overall economic growth. Thus, we consider in the next section of this chapter technology policies aimed at increasing private-sector investments in R&D.

It is difficult to demonstrate this same descriptive relationship for *comparative* (our emphasis) purposes across all countries using a panel of data and a simple and similar regression equation model specified as in equation (2.1) just above. The reason for this difficulty is that there are many institutional factors that are unique to each country that are not easily controlled for in such an empirical exercise. For us, being most familiar with the nature of investments in R&D in the United Kingdom and in the United States, this was not a problem although a visual inspection of the growth in the multi-factor productivity indices in Figure 2.7 and Figure 2.8 shows differences in the magnitude of the economic recessions (although we are aware that other country controls merit consideration as well).

In a second-best exploratory effort to make inferences about countries other than the United Kingdom and the United States, consider the growth in the multi-factor productivity index for year 2017 for the countries listed in Table 2.4. The associated Figure 2.9 shows both the growth in the multi-factor productivity index and the percent of each country's gross domestic investments in R&D in the private sector (in decimal terms). The correlation between these two metrics is 0.385. Even without accounting for cross-country controls for institutional factors that are unique to each country, the relationship between these two metrics mirrors the observation that investments in private-sector investments in R&D do matter, and (at the risk of inferring causation based only on descriptive statistics) those investments matter from a policy perspective for multi-factor productivity growth.

Table 2.4 *Growth in multi-factor productivity and the percent of gross domestic R&D financed by firms in the private sector for year 2017 for selected countries*

Country	Multi-Factor Productivity Growth (%)	Percent R&D (%)
Austria	0.573	54.65
Belgium	0.071	63.49
Canada	1.656	42.67
Denmark	0.666	58.52
Finland	2.181	58.01
France	1.620	56.078
Germany	1.180	66.18
Greece	0.177	44.77
Italy	0.854	53.69
Japan	1.470	78.2
Korea	2.556	76.23
Luxembourg	-1.404	49.58
Netherlands	1.052	51.63
New Zealand	-1.574	46.41
Norway	1.609	42.83
Portugal	0.508	46.51
Spain	0.878	47.79

Country	Multi-Factor Productivity Growth (%)	Percent R&D (%)
Sweden	0.272	60.76
Switzerland	1.430	67.04
United States	0.700	62.48

Source: https://stats.oecd.org/Index.aspx?QueryId=54567 (accessed October 20, 2020) and Table 2.2.

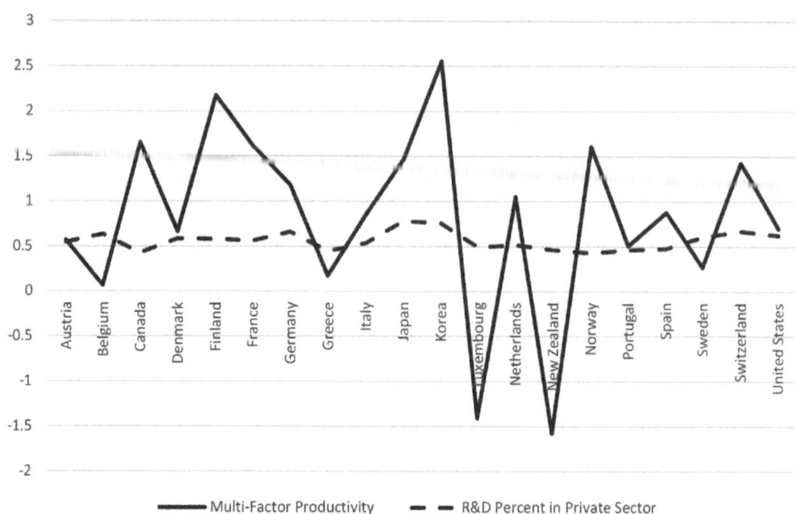

Source: Table 2.4.

Figure 2.9 *Growth in multi-factor productivity and the percent of gross domestic investments in R&D in the private sector for year 2017 for selected countries*

PRIVATE-SECTOR UNDERINVESTMENT IN R&D

There is a rich literature in economics and public policy that suggests that private-sector firms underinvest in R&D (see Arrow, 1962; Link and Scott, 2011; Mansfield, 1968, 1980; Tassey, 2004, 2017, 2019), and more generally the underinvestment is more pronounced in certain industrial sectors such as the U.S. energy sector and the Canadian agricultural sector (see Margolis and Kammen, 1999; Nemet and Kammen, 2007; Xiao and Fulton, 2018). An EU study by Duchêne et al. (2011) highlights the underinvestments in private-sector R&D, and the authors attribute the overall lower level of investments to sectoral specialization (see Moncada-Paternò-Castello et al., 2010).

Such underinvestments are due to the existence of investment barriers that bring about what is known by the term *market failure*.

Following Link and Scott (2001), there are at least eight categories of risk that firms face when making investments in R&D.[4] These non-mutually exclusive categories of risk, which can result in the expected private rate of return to the firm being less than the desired social rate of return from the use of R&D resources, are:

- High technical risk associated with the underlying R&D: the risk of the R&D project is greater than what the firm can accept, although if the R&D is successful there would be large benefits to society as a whole.
- High capital costs to undertake the underlying R&D: the R&D project may require too much financial and human capital for any one firm to expend, and thus the firm will not invest in the R&D project although society would be better off if it did.
- Long time to complete the R&D project and commercialize the resulting technology: the time expected to complete the R&D project and the time until commercialization of the R&D results are both long and variable, and thus a cash flow issue may overwhelm the firm and deter third-party investors.
- Underlying R&D spills over to multiple markets and is not appropriable: it is not uncommon for the scope of potential markets for the technology that results from the R&D project to be broader than the scope of the individual firm's market strategies so the firm will not perceive or project economic benefits from all potential market applications of the technology and thus the firm will underestimate the potential returns it can earn compared to the cost of the R&D project.
- Market success of the technology depends on technologies in different industries: markets evolve over time and thus R&D investments in a portfolio of projects might be needed but pursuit of such a portfolio might be beyond the financial and technical capabilities of the firm.
- Property rights cannot be assigned to the underlying R&D: not all property rights from any technology that results from the R&D project can be appropriated by the firm and thus might spill over to other firms especially competing firms.
- Resulting technology must be compatible and interoperable with other technologies: technology-based products are often part of larger systems of products, and that system might not exist or might not be mature when the initial R&D investment is made, hence there is a risk that the resulting technology might not be able to interface with other products in the market.

- High risk of opportunistic behavior when sharing information about the technology: there are situations that exist where the complexity of the R&D resulting technology requires an agreement on expected product performance between potential buyers and the firm, and such agreements have elements of uncertainty and thus are costly.

Individually, or in combination, these barriers to the potential development and marketability of any resulting technology lead private-sector firms to underinvest in R&D from the perspective of society. To mitigate against an underinvestment, policy makers need to consider technology policies that stimulate technological change from the supply side as well as from the demand side of the market (see Norberg-Bohm, 2000). Any technology policy must therefore remove or lessen these risk-related barriers noted above if private-sector investments in R&D are to be increased and thus productivity gains are to be realized.

TECHNOLOGY POLICY MECHANISMS

In this section, we discuss two technology policy mechanisms used by various governments to support private-sector investments in R&D. The first mechanism relates to tax incentives and the second mechanism relates to direct funding support.

Tax Incentives for Private-Sector R&D

Table 2.5 shows for year 2017 the percent of Gross Domestic Product (GDP) in the United Kingdom and in the United States that has been allocated as tax incentives and as direct R&D subsidies to all sectors of the respective countries. For comparative purposes, the relative technology policy emphasis in the United Kingdom is on tax incentives, and in the United States it is more balanced, but it leans toward the direction of direct R&D subsidies.

Table 2.5 Percent of Gross Domestic Product allocated to selected technology policies, years 2016 and 2017

	Percent of GDP	
Country	Tax Incentives (2016, %)	Direct Subsidies (2017, %)
United Kingdom	22.5	8.69
United States	8.05	12.79

Source: https://stats.oecd.org/Index.aspx?DataSetCode=RDTAX (accessed August 11, 2020).

Within the EU, different types of R&D tax incentives are used across Member States in order to support private-sector R&D (Table 2.6). The EC (2017a, pp. 11–12) outlined that some of the impacts of R&D tax incentives include increased private-sector investments in R&D, innovation development, and related activities in young innovative companies. There is an acknowledgement by the EC of the importance of design and implementation in relationship to effectiveness and use of best practices and of the administrative and compliance costs and burdens that R&D tax incentives can place on firms. In conclusion, the EC (2017a, pp. 14–15) noted:

> Currently, 25 Member States in the EU are using R&D tax incentives to stimulate business R&D in an effort to boost business R&D investment, increase productivity and economic growth. R&D incentives are becoming more popular for different reasons, for example because of their administrative simplicity and because they are neutral and provide a level playing field … Evidence suggests that the additionality effects are higher for SMEs and young companies … Good practices in the administration of R&D tax incentives include one-stop, online application procedures and guidelines for businesses, short time for tax authorities to make decisions on eligibility, assessors of the R&D tax incentives claims with expertise in the field, [and] use of risk-based control mechanisms. Governments should ensure that R&D tax incentive policies provide value for money through regular and rigorous evaluation, based on high-quality firm-level data.

However, based on a broad country study by the OECD (2019, p. 47), a number of pertinent policy considerations were suggested:

> The additionality of direct support for R&D appears to be slightly but not statistically significantly higher than for R&D tax incentives when analysed in a comparable fashion … A likely trade off arises between the ability to select the project with potentially highest additionality, and the ability to channel support to firms without directing the R&D activity while at the same time complying with international trade and competition rules. Direct measure of support can be better targeted towards activities, firms and areas where higher additionality and spillovers could be generated.

In practice, national governments use a range of tax incentives to support private-sector investments in R&D, as noted by the OECD (2018a, p. 9):

> Some R&D tax incentive schemes explicitly target specific types of R&D costs. Overall, there is a general preference for considering within the scope of eligible R&D costs those relating to labour and other current expenditures. R&D personnel costs account for the largest share of intramural R&D costs, and the focus on R&D personnel does in principle incentivise investment in human resources based in the domestic economy.

Table 2.6 *R&D tax incentive in the European Union, by country*

	Type of R&D Tax Incentive					Type of Tax		
	Expense-based Incentive				Input-based Incentive			
Country	Tax Credit	Enhanced Allowance	Accelerated Depreciation	Existing Expense-based	Patent Box	Corporate Income Tax	Personal Income Tax	Wage Tax/SSCs
Belgium	x	x	x	x	x	x		x
Bulgaria	x		x	x		x		
Czech Republic	x	x		x		x		
Denmark	x	x	x	x		x		
Germany								
Estonia								
Ireland	x			x	x	x		
Greece		x		x	x	x		
Spain	x			x	x	x		
France	x			x	x	x	x	x
Croatia		x		x		x		

	Type of R&D Tax Incentive					Type of Tax		
	Expense-based Incentive				Input-based Incentive			
Country	Tax Credit	Enhanced Allowance	Accelerated Depreciation	Existing Expense-based	Patent Box	Corporate Income Tax	Personal Income Tax	Wage Tax/SSCs
Italy	x		x	x	x	x		
Cyprus		x		x	x	x		
Latvia		x	x	x		x		
Lithuania		x	x	x		x		
Luxembourg					x	x	x	x
Hungary		x		x	x	x		x
Malta	x			x	x	x		
Netherlands	x	x		x	x	x	x	x
Austria	x			x		x	x	x
Poland	x	x	x	x		x	x	
Portugal	x			x	x	x		
Romania		x	x	x		x		

	Type of R&D Tax Incentive					Type of Tax		
	Expense-based Incentive				Input-based Incentive			
Country	Tax Credit	Enhanced Allowance	Accelerated Depreciation	Existing Expense-based	Patent Box	Corporate Income Tax	Personal Income Tax	Wage Tax/SSCs
Slovenia		x	x	x		x	x	
Slovakia		x		x		x		
Finland								
Sweden	x			x				x
United Kingdom	x	x	x	x	x	x		
Norway	x			x		x		
Canada	x		x	x		x	x	x
United States	x		x	x		x		
Israel	x	x	x	x		x		
Japan	x	x	x	x		x		

Source: https://op.europa.eu/en/publication-detail/-/publication/d9ae78f3-9f41-11e7-b92d-01aa75ed71a1/language-en, p. 6 (accessed October 20, 2020).
Note: SSC refers to Social Security Contributions. Patent Box refers to the taxation of patent revenues at a low rate to provide an incentive for greater investments in R&D.

When designing effective tax incentives aimed at increasing private-sector investments in R&D, governments and policy makers need to be mindful of a crowding out effect. A crowding out effect refers to the situation in which tax incentives may not stimulate the desired policy outcomes because the measures do not create sufficient incentives to overcome their impact on the national deficit and thus are rendered ineffective or inefficient. In other words, there is not the additionality that was anticipated by policy makers and their legislated efforts.

Various studies have examined crowding out effects in different country contexts: for France, see Marino et al. (2016); for Germany, see Hottenrott and Rexhäuser (2015); for Italy, see Cerulli and Potì (2012); and for the Netherlands, see Lokshin and Mohnen (2012). Such studies highlight the importance of policy incentive design and implementation.

Like any policy tool, tax incentives have advantages and disadvantages. The advantages include the following:[5]

- Tax incentives entail less interference in the marketplace than do many other mechanisms, thus affording private-sector recipients the ability to retain autonomy regarding the use of the incentives; tax incentives require less paperwork than other programs.
- Tax incentives eliminate the need to directly target individual firms in need of assistance; tax incentives have the psychological advantage of achieving a favorable industry reaction.
- Tax incentives may be permanent and thus do not require annual budget review.

There are also disadvantages associated with tax incentives:

- Tax incentives may bring about unintended windfalls by rewarding firms for what they would have done in the absence of the incentive.
- Tax incentives often result in undesirable inequities.
- Tax incentives raid the Federal treasury.
- Tax incentives frequently undermine public accountability.
- The effectiveness of tax incentives often varies over the business cycle.

Table 2.7 shows government support of private-sector investments in R&D through tax incentives as a percent of GDP, by country. The data in the table are for year 2016. The range of government support is large. The countries of Estonia, Finland, Germany, Luxembourg, Mexico, and Switzerland had in 2017 zero support of private-sector investments in R&D through tax incentives. (See the Tax Credit column in Table 2.6.) In the United States, tax incentives for private-sector investments in R&D were just over 8 percent of GDP compared to 22 percent in the United Kingdom. The upper bound of support is in Belgium at nearly 30 percent.

Table 2.7 *Government support of private-sector firm R&D through tax incentives in year 2016 as a percentage of Gross Domestic Product, by country*

Country	R&D Tax Incentives as a Percentage of GDP (%)
Australia	15.98
Austria	14.77
Belgium	29.95
Canada	13.45
Chile	1.09
Colombia	2.16
Czech Republic	5.01
Denmark	1.9
Estonia	0
Finland	0
France	28.33
Germany	0
Greece	0.77
Hungary	9.05
Iceland	6.25
Ireland	24.66
Italy	8.33
Japan	11.06
Korea	12.93
Latvia	0.26
Lithuania	2.58
Luxembourg	0
Mexico	0
Netherlands	17.05
New Zealand	0.51
Norway	12.04
Poland	0.21
Portugal	11.28
Slovak Republic	0.45
Slovenia	11.27
Spain	3.23
Sweden	1.16
Switzerland	0
Turkey	5.7
United Kingdom	22.50
United States	8.05

Source: https://stats.oecd.org/Index.aspx?DataSetCode=RDTAX (accessed August 11, 2020).
Note: Year 2016 is reported because of missing data for year 2017 for several countries.

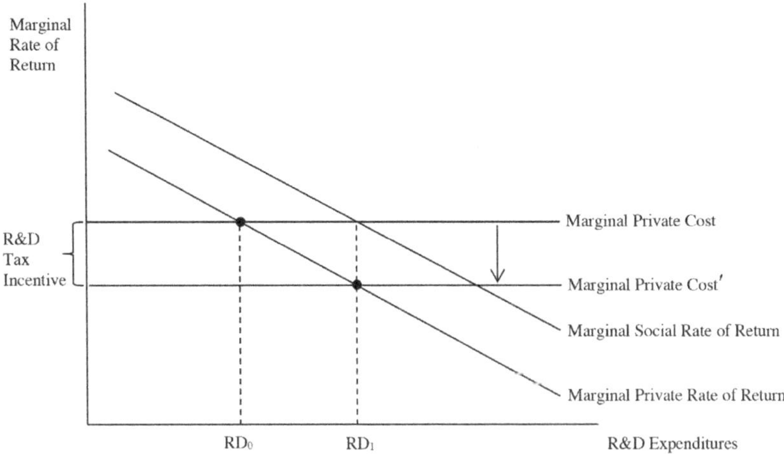

Source: Based on Leyden and Link (2015).

Figure 2.10 The economics of an R&D tax incentive

Figure 2.10 illustrates the economics implications of a tax incentive for private-sector investments in R&D. Measured on the vertical axis is the marginal rate of return to private-sector investments in R&D, and measured on the horizontal axis are different levels of private-sector investments in R&D. Both the marginal social rate of return and the marginal private rate of return schedules are downward sloping reflecting diminishing returns to R&D investments for a given time horizon.

The social rate of return schedule in Figure 2.10 is drawn as being greater than the private rate of return schedule for all investment levels of R&D. The rationale for the social rate of return schedule being greater than the private rate of return schedule follows from the assumption that private-sector firms cannot appropriate all the benefits from their investments in R&D, which is also a barrier leading to private-sector firms underinvesting in R&D from a social perspective—some of those benefits spill over to other firms in the current time period and in the post-innovation time period, thus generating additional benefits to society. Completing the figure, the marginal private cost to the private-sector firm to undertake additional investments in R&D, conceptualized as the opportunity cost of R&D investments (e.g., x%), is assumed to be constant; the marginal private cost schedule is thus drawn as a horizontal line.

In equilibrium, the private-sector firm will equate the marginal private cost of conducting R&D with the marginal private rate of return associated with the R&D activity, and the private profit-maximizing level of R&D for the firm is at the investment level RD_0 (Marginal Private Cost = Marginal Private Rate of Return) in Figure 2.10. However, the social profit-maximizing level of R&D is for the firm to invest at the level RD_1 (Marginal Private Cost = Marginal Social Rate of Return) in Figure 2.10.

Society, given the firm's marginal private cost schedule, would like the firm to invest in R&D to maximize social benefits. Thus, the optimal tax incentive is one that provides an incentive to the private-sector firm to increase its investments in R&D from RD_0 to RD_1.

If the private-sector firm's marginal private cost of conducting R&D were lower, and thus would be in Figure 2.10 at Marginal Private Cost′, the profit-maximizing level of R&D for the firm would be at the investment level RD_1 (Marginal Private Cost′ = Marginal Private Rate of Return) in Figure 2.10. Thus, the relevant technology policy question is: How can the government decrease the marginal private cost of R&D in private-sector firms?

In the United Kingdom, three tax-related policy tools are used for reducing the marginal private cost of R&D in private-sector firms: a tax credit for R&D, an R&D expenditure credit, and an R&D depreciation allowance. In the United States, there is one primary tax-related policy tool, a tax credit for R&E (research and experimentation expenditures).[6,7] The institutional details of these tax incentives for both countries are outlined in the OECD's report, *OECD Compendium of Information on R&D Tax Incentives, 2019* (OECD, 2019), and in the OECD's report, *OECD R&D Tax Incentive Database* (OECD, 2020). The details of tax incentives for the other OECD countries are also outlined in these two reports.[8]

Direct Subsidies of Private-Sector R&D

Table 2.8 provides an overview of government support of private-sector firm R&D through direct R&D subsidies as a percent of GDP, by country. The data in Table 2.8 are for year 2017. The range of subsidy support is broad. For example, the level of subsidy support in Lithuania is less than one-half of 1 percent; in the United Kingdom, the level of support is nearly 9 percent; and in the United States the level of support is more than 12 percent. Korea's support of private-sector R&D through direct subsidies is just over 16 percent of its GDP.

Table 2.8 *Government support of private-sector firm R&D through direct subsidies as a percentage of Gross Domestic Product for year 2017, by country*

Country	Direct Subsidy as a Percent of GDP (%)
Australia	2.26
Austria	7.83
Belgium	6.3
Canada	5.65
Chile	1.58
Czech Republic	7.91
Denmark	4.0
Estonia	2.67
Finland	5.55
France	11.52
Germany	6.72
Greece	2.25
Hungary	13.22
Iceland	12.39
Ireland	4.29
Israel	11.45
Italy	2.99
Japan	2.33
Korea	16.01
Latvia	0.86
Lithuania	0.4
Luxembourg	4.63
Mexico	1.36
Netherlands	2.44
New Zealand	8.98
Norway	10.38
Poland	9.28
Portugal	2.81
Slovak Republic	1.18
Slovenia	7.4
Spain	5.82
Sweden	11.28
Switzerland	2.33
Turkey	4.89
United Kingdom	8.69
United States	12.79

Source: https://stats.oecd.org/Index.aspx?DataSetCode=RDTAX (accessed August 12, 2020).

Arguably, the hallmark technology policy program to provide direct financial support to private-sector firms—small private-sector firms in particular—to conduct R&D is the U.S. Small Business Innovation Research (SBIR) program. The SBIR program was created in the United States through the Small Business Innovation Development Act of 1982. This legislation was one of several legislations promulgated in the United States in the early 1980s in response to the productivity slowdown that plagued the U.S. economy (see Figure 1.2 in Chapter 1).

The U.S. SBIR program is a set-aside program. Agencies are required to set aside a portion of their extramural R&D research budget and to allocate those funds to small firms (less than 500 employees) to conduct targeted agency-specific research projects. The current set-aside rate is 3.2 percent.

The current mission of the U.S. SBIR program is:[9]

> … to support scientific excellence and technological innovation through the investment of Federal research funds in critical American priorities to build a strong national economy.

The program's current goals are to:

- Stimulate technological innovation.
- Meet Federal research and development needs.
- Foster and encourage participation in innovation and entrepreneurship by women and socially or economically disadvantaged persons.
- Increase private-sector commercialization of innovations derived from Federal research and development funding.

More details about the U.S. SBIR program are presented in Chapter 4.

Much has been written about the U.S. SBIR program, and in particular about the success of the program in increasing the rate of commercialization of new technologies funded through the program (see Link, 2013). However, little has been written about the diffusion of the SBIR program concept to other countries.

A comparable program in the United Kingdom is the Small Business Research Initiative (SBRI), and it was initiated in 2001 to mirror the U.S. SBIR program (Manchester Institute of Innovation Research, 2015, pp. 15, 24):

> The UK Government's Small Business Research Initiative (SBRI) programme is one of a number of precommercial procurement programmes (PCP) that have been developed internationally and which are based on the US Government's Small Business Innovation Research (SBIR) programme introduced in 1982.
>
> The UK programme has two main objectives: a) supporting Government departments in finding solutions to their own policy / operational needs where current solutions are inadequate or don't exist, and b) to support technological development

> amongst firms. Government policy objectives can include the development of technology for private users where there is a public policy rationale. To the extent that the programme attempts to define through an SBRI procurement (of R&D services) how a need may be met, the SBRI is an example of a so-called demand side measure. The emphasis of the SBRI is upon meeting the needs of government through novelty and the issue of a challenge to industry rather than simply the development of technology in itself.

The U.K. SBRI program was later considered a major failure due to the fact it did not emulate the performance success of the U.S. SBIR program. By 2007 further changes were made to the existing SBRI program (see Tredgett and Coad, 2014). Tredgett and Coad (2014) undertook an analysis to assess the performance of the U.K. SBRI program over its first three years against the U.S. SBIR program. For the purposes of their analysis and evaluation, the authors considered years 1983 through 1985 in the United States and years 2009 through 2011 in the United Kingdom. In the United States, Phase I proof of concept awards increased by 694 during the period 1983 through 1985 while in the United Kingdom Phase I awards decreased by 56. Over these same time periods, Phase II technology development awards in the United States increased by 346, and in the United Kingdom they only increased by 8.[10] See Table 2.9.

Table 2.9 Comparison of number of SBRI program awards in the United Kingdom and number of SBIR program awards in the United States

	Year 1	Year 2	Year 3
U.S. SBIR Phase I Awards	789	1016	1483
U.K. SBRI Phase I Awards	328	124	272
U.S. SBIR Phase II Awards	227	356	573
U.K. SBRI Phase II Awards	5	104	13

Source: Based on Tredgett and Coad (2014).
Note: Years 1 through 3 in the table refer to years 1983 through 1985 in the United States and years 2009 through 2011 in the United Kingdom.

The U.S. SBIR program had more Phase I and Phase II awards being made in comparison to the U.K. SBRI program. The monetary value was also greater for the U.S. awards than for the U.K. SBRI awards. While the amount of Phase I and Phase II U.K. awards is similar, there is a sizeable difference between Phase I and Phase II awards under the U.S. SBIR program, with Phase II awards being the greater. See Table 2.10.

Table 2.10 Comparison of award amounts of the SBRI program in the United Kingdom and the SBIR program awards in the United States (£ 000s)

	Year 1	Year 2	Year 3
U.S. SBIR Phase I Awards	52,431	66,132	100,193
U.K. SBRI Phase I Awards	12,706	6,360	19,242
U.S. SBIR Phase II Awards	0	134,810	162,794
U.K. SBRI Awards	2,808	17,457	1,930

Source: Based on Tredgett and Coad (2014).
Note: Years 1 through 3 in the table refer to years 1983 through 1985 in the United States and years 2009 through 2011 in the United Kingdom.

Table 2.11 shows the dates when other countries adopted programs aimed at small firms like the U.S. SBIR program.

Table 2.11 International adoption of programs similar to the U.S. SBIR Program

Country	Year of Adoption
United States	1982
South Africa	1993
Turkey	1995
Australia	1996
South Korea	1998
Japan	1999
Taiwan	1999
United Kingdom	2001
Netherlands	2005
New Zealand	2012

Source: We thank Thorsten Gores for his able research assistance in the preparation of this table.

CONCLUDING OBSERVATIONS

Gross domestic investments in R&D by private-sector firms are the major target variable of technology policy in most countries because such investments have a *direct* (our emphasis) impact on productivity and economic growth. This impact varies by country.

In Chapter 3 and Chapter 4, we investigate, in a descriptive way, the effectiveness of technology policies across countries. Then, in Chapter 5, we discuss what we refer to as elements of the technology policy environment, that is, the environmental factors that leverage the impact that investments in private-sector R&D have on productivity and economic growth. These elements in each country are the patent system and the incentive for firms to engage in collaborative R&D.

NOTES

1. There are missing data for some years in the OECD dataset from which these percentages came.
2. The foundational research on this topic traces to Minasian (1969), Terleckyj (1974), Mansfield (1980), Link (1981), and Griliches (1986). As more complete datasets evolved over time, and as econometric models evolved a host of studies on this topic were completed and their emphasis was on U.S. private-sector firms as well as international private-sector firms (see Hall et al., 2010).
3. These levels of significance are based on t-statistics calculated using heteroscedasticity-consistent (i.e., robust) standard errors. Autocorrelation is not a statistical issue.
4. The remainder of this section follows directly from Link and Scott (2001).
5. This section follows directly from Bozeman and Link (1984) and Leyden and Link (2015).
6. There is a distinction, from a U.S. National Science Foundation (NSF) reporting perspective and from a tax credit perspective, between R&D expenditures and R&E expenditures. R&E expenditures are somewhat more narrowly defined to include all costs incident to development. R&E does not include ordinary testing or inspection of materials or products for quality control of those for efficiency studies, etc. R&E, in a sense, is the experimental portion of R&D. Given this definitional and reporting distinction between R&D and R&E, we believe that it is fair to say that most policy makers in the United States will simply make reference to the "R&D tax credit."
7. See Leyden and Link (2015) and Link and Cunningham (2021) for a discussion of the Economic Recovery Tax Act of 1981 (ERTA).

8. One of the earliest cross-country comparisons of R&D tax credits is in Leyden and Link (1993). This publication was one of several fundamental studies that led to the OECD's continuing efforts to study R&D tax credits across countries (see Guinet and Kamata, 1996).
9. See https://www.sbir.gov/about (accessed July 20, 2020).
10. Phase I and Phase II awards are discussed in greater detail in Chapter 4.

3. The effectiveness of technology policy

In Chapter 2, we described technology policies to enhance private-sector investments in R&D, and the technology policies that we emphasized are tax incentives and direct subsidies. The question of effectiveness of technology policy (and innovation policy) is always a predominant consideration and focus for policy makers. A general question that they ask is: Do policy interventions yield the desired behavioral changes at the firm level, and does the firm realize the envisaged performance? The question that we ask in this chapter is more specific, namely: How effective have tax incentives and direct subsidies been to increase the level of private-sector R&D?

We also proffered in Chapter 2 that policy makers are concerned with evaluating policy effectiveness and how the policy mix that they have implemented has stimulated and supported private-sector investments in R&D. Here, we offer some suggestive evidence from an exploratory descriptive cross-country analysis about these two issues.

Figure 3.1 presents a framework for our study of technology and innovation policy. Recall that we introduced a paradigm in Chapter 1 for the themes in this book. We suggested:

R&D → technology → innovation → economic growth

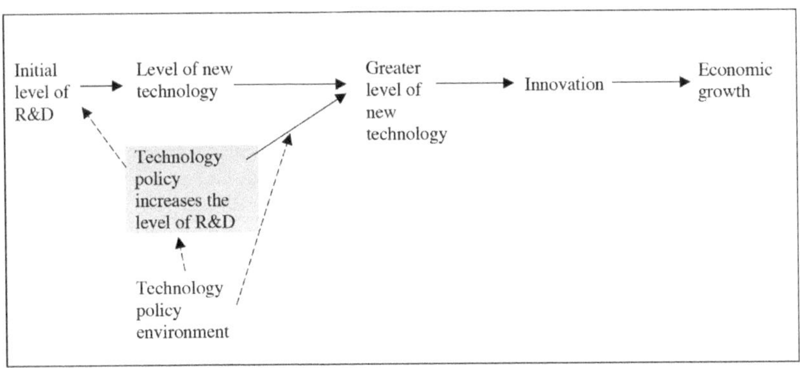

Source: Prepared by the authors.

Figure 3.1 *Framework for explaining the role of investments in R&D and the role of technology policy and innovation policy in the economy*

Figure 3.1 expands on that paradigm by illustrating in more detail the *technology* → *innovation* steps from a policy perspective.

We will discuss the framework in Figure 3.1 in several of the following chapters, and thus the framework will serve as a unifying construct for the topics presented in this book. In this chapter, we focus on the shaded cell labeled as "Technology policy increases the level of R&D," and on the dashed line from that cell to the cell labeled as "Initial level of R&D."

Tables 3.1, 3.2, and 3.3 are reproduced, in part, from tables in Chapter 2. In their abbreviated form, the same 34 countries are listed in each table. To address the research question about the effectiveness of tax incentives and direct subsidies to increase the level of private-sector R&D, we considered a model of the general form:

$$R\&D = f\,(TaxIncentives,\ R\&DSubsidies) \tag{3.1}$$

The data for measuring the variable *R&D* by country come from Table 3.1, the data for measuring the variable *TaxIncentives* come from Table 3.2, and the data for measuring the variable *R&DSubsidies* come from Table 3.3. Estimates from regression specifications of the model in equation (3.1) provide suggestive information about the relationship between a change in *TaxIncentives* and a change in *R&D*, and on the relationship between a change in *R&DSubsidies* and a change in *R&D*. The data in Tables 3.1 through 3.3 are not sufficiently rich for lag patterns to be considered; thus, the descriptive regression findings presented in this chapter are suggestive and should be viewed as such.

A priori, if the policy intent of tax incentives to increase private-sector R&D and of direct R&D subsidies to increase private-sector R&D are well designed, and if the mechanisms across countries are well structured, the regression coefficient on each of the independent variables should be positive. In other words, this empirical exercise will inform the relationship between the two alternative technology policies and the level of private-sector investment in R&D from a cross-country perspective.

Table 3.1 Percent of gross domestic R&D financed by firms in the private sector, by country for year 2017

Country	Percent (%)
Austria	54.65
Belgium	63.49
Canada	42.67
Chile	31.43
Czech Republic	39.32
Denmark	58.52
Estonia	43.57
Finland	58.01
France	56.08
Germany	66.18
Greece	44.77
Hungary	52.68
Iceland	36.42
Ireland	*48.99*
Italy	53.68
Japan	78.27
Korea	76.23
Latvia	24.15
Lithuania	35.42
Luxembourg	49.58
Mexico	19.05
Netherlands	51.63
New Zealand	46.40
Norway	42.83
Poland	52.54
Portugal	46.51
Slovak Republic	49.03
Slovenia	63.15
Spain	47.79
Sweden	60.76
Switzerland	67.04
Turkey	49.45
United Kingdom	*51.77*
United States	62.48

Source: https://www.oecd.org/sti/inno/researchanddevelopmentstatisticsrds.htm (accessed October 20, 2020). Presented in Chapter 2 as Table 2.2.
Note: Values in italics are for year 2016.

Table 3.2 *Government support of private-sector firm R&D through tax incentives for year 2016 as a percentage of Gross Domestic Product, by country*

Country	R&D Tax Incentives as a Percentage of GDP (%)
Austria	14.77
Belgium	29.95
Canada	13.45
Chile	1.09
Czech Republic	5.01
Denmark	1.9
Estonia	0
Finland	0
France	28.33
Germany	0
Greece	0.77
Hungary	9.05
Iceland	6.25
Ireland	24.66
Italy	8.33
Japan	11.06
Korea	12.93
Latvia	0.26
Lithuania	2.58
Luxembourg	0
Mexico	0
Netherlands	17.05
New Zealand	0.51
Norway	12.04
Poland	0.21
Portugal	11.28
Slovak Republic	0.45
Slovenia	11.27
Spain	3.23
Sweden	1.16
Switzerland	0
Turkey	5.7
United Kingdom	22.50
United States	8.05

Source: https://stats.oecd.org/Index.aspx?DataSetCode=RDTAX (accessed August 11, 2020). Presented in Chapter 2 as Table 2.7.
Note: Year 2016 is reported because of missing 2017 data for several countries.

Table 3.3 Government support of private-sector firm R&D through direct subsidies as a percentage of Gross Domestic Product for year 2017, by country

Country	Direct Subsidy as a Percent of GDP (%)
Austria	7.83
Belgium	6.3
Canada	5.65
Chile	1.58
Czech Republic	7.91
Denmark	4.0
Estonia	2.67
Finland	5.55
France	11.52
Germany	6.72
Greece	2.25
Hungary	13.22
Iceland	12.39
Ireland	4.29
Italy	2.99
Japan	2.33
Korea	16.01
Latvia	0.86
Lithuania	0.4
Luxembourg	4.63
Mexico	1.36
Netherlands	2.44
New Zealand	8.98
Norway	10.38
Poland	9.28
Portugal	2.81
Slovak Republic	1.18
Slovenia	7.4
Spain	5.82
Sweden	11.28
Switzerland	2.33
Turkey	4.89
United Kingdom	8.69
United States	12.79

Source: https://stats.oecd.org/Index.aspx?DataSetCode=RDTAX (accessed August 12, 2020). Presented in Chapter 2 as Table 2.8.

We estimated four regression models:

- The first model regressed the actual tax incentive and R&D subsidy data in Tables 3.2 and 3.3, respectively, on the R&D data in Table 3.1. In this model, n = 34.
- In the second model, the dependent variable and the independent variables are measured in logarithmic terms. In this model, country data observations on *TaxIncentives* were changed from 0 to 0.001 so that logarithms of those country observations were measurable. A binary variable equal to 1 was also included as a regressor for those country observations with *TaxIncentives* values of 0 changed to 0.001, and 0 otherwise. In this model, n = 34.
- The third model deleted country observations for which *TaxIncentives* equals 0. The dependent variable and the independent variables are as represented in the tables. For this model, n = 28.
- The fourth model is the same as the third model except that all of the variables are measured in logarithmic terms. For this model, n = 28.

For every model, the estimated regression coefficients on the *TaxIncentives* variables are positive but not statistically significant at a conventional level. For every model, the estimated regression coefficients on the *R&DSubsidy* variables are positive and statistically significant at the 0.10 level or better. In the first and third models, the estimated coefficient on *R&DSubsidy* was approximately 0.9 meaning that an increase of 10 percentage points in direct R&D subsidies as a percentage of GDP is associated with an increase of 9 percentage points in the percent of gross domestic R&D financed by firms in the private sector.

Our interpretation of these descriptive findings, albeit that they are based on a small cross-sectional sample of countries, is that both tax incentives and R&D direct subsidies do matter when it comes to being related to a country's investments in R&D (i.e., both technology policies are effective as evidenced by positive regression coefficients), but R&D direct subsidies matter more in an absolute sense as well as in a statistical sense (i.e., a direct R&D subsidy technology policy is effective as well as more efficient). Furthermore, these findings anticipate the question about how interdependent technology policies and innovation policies are with other government policies (a topic that is beyond the scope of this book, however).

In Chapter 4, we continue to explore dimensions of the effectiveness of direct subsidies to R&D. Specifically, we focus on the U.S. SBIR program, and we suggest that this technology policy program has unanticipated consequences which may give pause to some U.S. policy makers and may provide insight to policy makers in other countries that have adopted SBIR-like programs (see Table 2.11).

4. Unanticipated consequences of technology policy

THE OBJECTIVE FUNCTION OF POLICY MAKERS

What do policy makers or legislators think about when crafting and adopting a new legislative initiative or modifying an existing legislative initiative?

One might begin to answer this question by accepting some initial assumptions. At one end of a so-called assumption spectrum is the proposition that the objective function of a legislator is to act in a manner that maximizes his or her probability of being re-elected to public office. The policy focus of policy makers is guided by legislated government actions. At the other end of this so-called assumption spectrum is the proposition that the objective function of a policy maker and legislator is to act in a manner that maximizes the public or social good. Countries have different legislative processes and institutions that support legislators. Of course, a legislator might believe that being re-elected to public office maximizes the public or social good! Therefore, such a myopic orientation might result in shorter term-oriented policy interventions and cycles. Regardless of where most policy makers or legislators fall along this assumption spectrum, there will likely be anticipated as well as unanticipated consequences to any and all of their legislated actions.

The concept of unanticipated consequences of an action traces at least to the writings of Frédéric Bastiat.[1] He wrote in 1848 in *Selected Essays on Political Economy* (1995, p. 1, emphases in the original):

> In the economic sphere an act, a habit, an institution, a law produces not only one effect, but a series of effects. Of these effects, the first alone is immediate; it appears simultaneously with its cause; *it is seen.* The other effects emerge only subsequently; *they are not seen;* we are fortunate if we *foresee* them.
>
> There is only one difference between a bad economist and a good one: the bad economist confines himself to the *visible* effect; the good economist takes into account both the effect that can be seen and those effects that must be *foreseen.*
>
> Yet this difference is tremendous; for it almost always happens that when the immediate consequence is favorable, the later consequences are disastrous, and vice versa. Whence it follows that the bad economist pursues a small present good that will be followed by a great evil to come, while the good economist pursues a great good to come, at the risk of a small present evil.

Bastiat went on to write that through experience one learns … one eventually learns to foresee consequences (1995, p. 2):

> Experience teaches efficaciously but brutally. It instructs us in all the effects of an act by making us feel them, and we cannot fail to learn eventually, from having been burned ourselves, that fire burns. I should prefer, in so far as possible, to replace this rude teacher with one more gentle: foresight.

Perhaps, then, based on Bastiat, in the world of legislative initiatives, the more experienced policy makers or members of a legislative group have more foresight than those with less experience. But, given that group dynamics are what they are, it is not always the more experienced policy maker or member of a legislative group whose voice is the loudest; and it is not always the case that experience is positively correlated with persuasiveness.

The eminent sociologist Robert Merton wrote in his famous essay "The Unanticipated Consequences of Purposive Social Action" the following (1936, p. 898):[2]

> The most obvious limitation to a correct anticipation of consequences of action is provided by the existing state of knowledge. The extent of this limitation may be best appreciated by assuming the simplest case where this lack of adequate knowledge is the sole barrier to a correct anticipation.

We suggest that there are anticipated as well as unanticipated consequences associated with policy makers' and legislators' actions related, within the context of this book, to technology policies. Some of the anticipated consequences have already been discussed in Chapters 2 and 3, and the implications of these anticipated consequences are illustrated in the framework presented in Figure 3.1 (reproduced here as Figure 4.1). Basically, an effective technology policy provides incentives for private-sector firms to increase their investments in R&D; investments in R&D are the target variable for technology policies as we have explicitly represented, starting in Chapter 1 with the paradigm:

$$R\&D \rightarrow technology \rightarrow innovation \rightarrow economic\ growth$$

The anticipated consequences of technology policy are innovation and subsequent economic growth. This, in turn, can benefit private-sector firms as well as contribute to the public or social good. However, there could be unanticipated consequences associated with private-sector firms increasing their investments in R&D, and we describe such consequences conceptually as well as quantitatively in the remainder of this chapter.

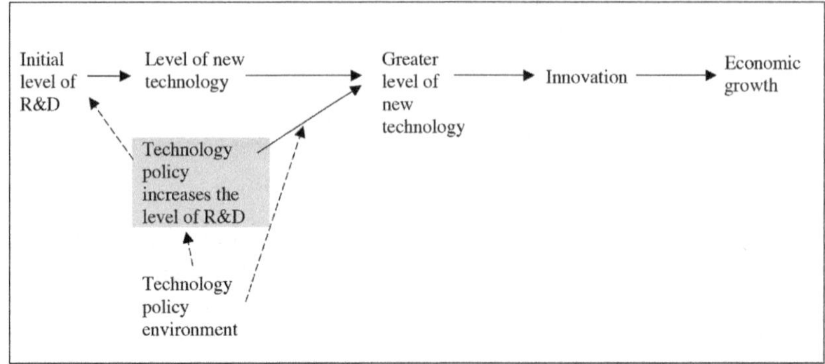

Source: Prepared by the authors.

Figure 4.1 *Framework for explaining the role of investments in R&D and the role of technology policy and innovation policy in the economy*

AN ILLUSTRATION OF UNANTICIPATED CONSEQUENCES

As background, consider Figure 4.2 which relates to a firm's investments in R&D. Assume technology policy is initiated either through an R&D tax incentive or through a direct R&D subsidy, and as a result of these policies the firm increases its investments in R&D from RD_0 to RD_1. Such investment response decisions are strategic for a firm because they entail risks and uncertainties.

The firm had established, as part of its investment decision-making strategy, what is generally referred to as a private hurdle rate. This private hurdle rate is the minimum expected rate of return that the firm must earn to justify the decision to invest at a given level of R&D (or more generally at a given level of per se investment). As shown in Figure 4.2, the expected rate of return from an investment in R&D in the amount RD_1 is above the firm's private hurdle rate, and thus the firm will find it in its financial interest to invest at least the amount of R&D that corresponds to RD_1.

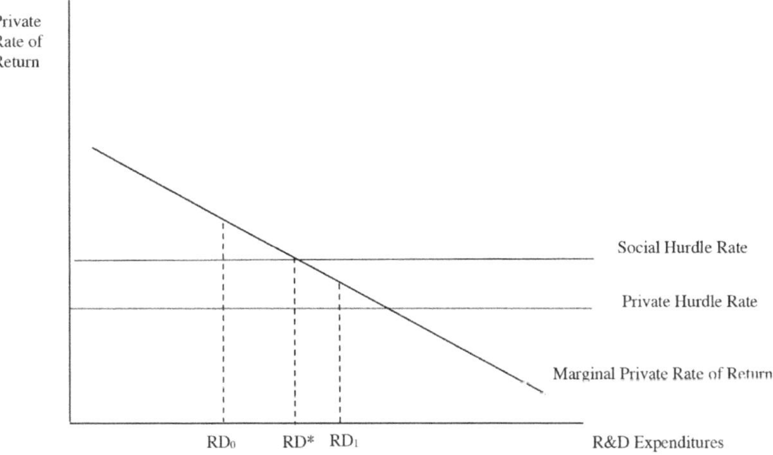

Figure 4.2 *Unanticipated consequences from a technology policy*

However, society also has a hurdle rate. The social hurdle rate is the minimum expected rate of return that society must earn to have its scarce resources invested in an R&D project. Such a hurdle rate has been considered against other demands and needs that legislators and policy makers have to consider from the perspective of a variety of policy arenas such as social security, health, education, defense, transportation, and so forth. As shown in Figure 4.2, the social hurdle rate is greater than the rate of return the firm expects to earn from an investment in R&D in the amount of RD_1. Thus, society would not want the firm to allocate RD_1 amount of R&D. In fact, society would not want the firm to invest in any amount of R&D that is greater than RD*.

A firm investing an amount of R&D equal to RD_1 represents a situation where the allocation of its resources in response to a technology policy was too large of an investment, and as a result the unanticipated consequences are, from society's perspective, a misallocation of resources.[3] The socially optimal technology policy would have been one that resulted in the firm increasing its investments in R&D from RD_0 to RD*.

The U.S. SBIR program was introduced in Chapter 2, and it is discussed here in more detail than in Chapter 2 in an effort to provide context for the illustration of unanticipated consequences that follows in this chapter.

The Legislative History of the SBIR Program[4]

The SBIR program is arguably a crown jewel of U.S. technology and innovation policy that is aimed at small firms and one that has been imitated in other countries (see Link and Cunningham, 2021). Regarding the modern genesis of the policy emphasis on small firms, one might begin with an emphasis on President Jimmy Carter's Domestic Policy Review (1979). This policy review was a response to the productivity slowdown that affected the U.S. manufacturing sector in the early 1970s, and then resurfaced in the late 1970s and early 1980s. See Chapter 1.

President Carter's emphasis on the role of small firms in the economy traces to an even earlier policy emphasis on small firms in the U.S. Small Business Act of 1953, Public Law 85–536:

> It is the declared policy of the Congress that the Federal Government … should aid and assist small businesses, as defined under this Act, to increase their ability to compete in international markets by—(A) enhancing their ability to export; (B) facilitating technology transfers; (C) enhancing their ability to compete effectively and efficiently against imports; (D) increasing the access of small businesses to long-term capital for the purchase of new plant and equipment used in the production of goods and services involved in international trade; (E) disseminating information concerning State, Federal, and private programs and initiatives to enhance the ability of small businesses to compete in international markets; and (F) ensuring that the interests of small businesses are adequately represented in bilateral and multilateral trade negotiations.

Drawing directly from President Carter's Domestic Policy Review (1979, p. 63):

> Industrial innovation—the development and commercialization of new products and processes—is an essential element of a strong and growing American economy. It helps ensure economic vitality, improved productivity, international competitiveness, job creation, and an improved quality of life for every American … America has been the world leader in developing new products, new processes, and new technologies, and in ensuring their wide dissemination and use … I am today announcing measures which will help ensure our country's continued role as the world leader in industrial innovation. [One of these measures or initiatives is in the area of] fostering the development of small innovative firms.

Specific to the development of small innovative firms, President Carter also noted (1979, p. 65):

> Small innovative firms have historically played an important role in bringing new technologies into the marketplace … First, I propose the enhancement by $10 million of the Small Business Innovation Research Program of the National Science Foundation. [T]he National Science Foundation will assist other agencies in implementing similar programs, with total Federal support eventually reaching $150 million per year.

The reference by President Carter to the National Science Foundation (NSF) is an acknowledgement of an earlier publicly supported research program focused on small firms.[5]

Shortly after the President's Domestic Policy Review, the Small Business Innovation Development Act of 1982, Public Law 97–219, was passed by Congress.[6] The goals of this legislative act, as stated in the Public Law, are:

(1) to stimulate technological innovation;
(2) to use small business to meet Federal research and development needs;
(3) to foster and encourage participation by minority and disadvantaged persons in technological innovation; and
(4) to increase private sector commercialization innovations derived from Federal research and development.

To raise funds to support these goals, the 1982 Act states that:

> Each Federal agency which has an extramural budget for research or research and development in excess of $100,000,000 for fiscal year 1982, or any fiscal year thereafter, shall expend not less than 0.2 per centum of its extramural budget in fiscal year 1983 or in such subsequent fiscal year as the agency has such budget, not less than 0.6 per centum of such budget in the second fiscal year thereafter; not less than 1 per centum of such budget in the third fiscal year thereafter, and not less than 1.25 per centum of such budget in all subsequent fiscal years with small business concerns specifically in connection with a small business innovation research program which meets the requirements of the Small Business Innovation Development Act of 1982 and regulations issued thereunder.

The SBIR program was created through the 1982 Act.[7] Three phases are defined in the 1982 Act, two of which pertain to SBIR funding. Phase I awards are designed to be small, proof of concept awards generally in amounts at that time not being over $50,000, and generally the projects are expected to last no longer than six months. The purpose of Phase I research awards is to assist firms investigate the feasibility of an idea's scientific potential in response to the funding agency's objectives. As specified in the 1982 Act, Phase I is:

> … a first phase for determining, insofar as possible, the scientific and technical merit and feasibility of ideas submitted pursuant to SBIR Program solicitations.

Phase II awards were originally capped at $500,000, and the projects were and still are expected to last for two years. The purpose of these awards is to develop further the proposed research, ideally leading to a commercializable product, process, or service. According to the 1982 Act, Phase II is:

> …a second phase to further develop the proposed ideas to meet the particular program needs, the awarding of which shall take into consideration the scientific

> and technical merit and feasibility evidenced by the first phase and, where two or more proposals are evaluated as being of approximately equal scientific and technical merit and feasibility, special consideration shall be given to those proposals that have demonstrated third phase, non-Federal capital commitments.

The firm receiving the SBIR Phase II award is expected to undertake further research on the funded project during what is referred to as Phase III. This is the phase during which the SBIR funded firm is expected to seek third party funding (e.g., angel funding and/or venture capital funding) to ensure that the product, process, or service developed during Phase II moves into the marketplace. According to the 1982 Act, Phase III is:

> … a third phase in which non-Federal capital pursues commercial applications of the research or research and development and which may also involve follow-on non-SBIR funded production contracts with a Federal agency for products or processes intended for use by the United States Government.

As stated in the 1982 Act, there are criteria for a firm to be eligible for an SBIR award. The firm must be: independently owned and operated; other than the dominant firm in the field in which it is proposing to carry out SBIR projects; organized and operated for profit; the employer of 500 or fewer employees, including employees of subsidiaries and affiliates; the primary source of employment for the project's principal investigator at the time of award and during the period when the research is conducted; and at least 51 percent owned by U.S. citizens or lawfully admitted permanent resident aliens.

Congress has periodically reauthorized the 1982 Act. The Act was not legislated to be permanent; accordingly, it has been revised and then reauthorized a number of times. A reauthorization timeline for the SBIR program since 1982 is (see Leyden and Link, 2015):

- In 1986, the 1982 Act was extended through 1992 as a part of the Department of Defense Appropriation Act of 1986, Public Law 99–443.
- In 1992, the SBIR program was reauthorized again until 2000 through the Small Business Research and Development Enactment Act, Public Law 102–564. The 1992 reauthorization also modified the structure of the SBIR program; it increased the maximum set-aside rate from 1.25 percent to 2.50 percent and re-emphasized the commercialization intent of SBIR funded technologies—see point (4) of the program's purpose statement above from the 1982 Act. The reauthorization also increased Phase I awards to \$100,000 and Phase II awards to \$750,000, and broadened above program objective (3) from the 1982 Act to also focus on women: "to provide for enhanced outreach efforts to increase the participation of … small businesses that are 51 percent owned and controlled by women."

- The Small Business Reauthorization Act of 2000, Public Law 106–554, extended the SBIR program until September 30, 2008, kept the 2.50 percent set aside, and did not increase the maximum amounts of Phase I and Phase II awards.
- Congress did not reauthorize the SBIR program by the legislated date of September 30, 2008; rather, Congress temporarily extended the program until March 20, 2009 with Public Law 110–235. The Senate version of the failed reauthorization bill (S. 3029) included, among other things, an increase in Phase I funding to $150,000 and an increase in Phase 2 funding to $1,000,000 with provisions for these funding guidelines to be exceeded by 50 percent. Also, the current 2.50 percent set aside would have increased to 3.50 percent at a rate of 0.10 percent per year over ten years, except for the National Institutes of Health which would have stayed at 2.50 percent.
- On March 19, 2009, the House and Senate reauthorized the SBIR program until July 31, 2009, Public Law 110–10.
- The SBIR program was again reauthorized until September 30, 2009 through a Senate continuing resolution, S. 1513.
- On September 23, 2009 House bill H.R. 3614 extended SBIR until October 31, 2009.
- Senate bill S. 1929 again extended the SBIR program until April 30, 2010.
- Senate bill S. 3253 extended the SBIR program to July 31.
- House bill H.R. 5849 extended the SBIR program to September 30, 2010.
- Senate bill S. 3839 extended the SBIR program to January 31, 2011.
- House bill H.R. 366 extended the SBIR program to May 31, 2011.
- Senate bill S. 1082, The Small Business Additional Extension Act of 2011, extended the SBIR program through September 30, 2011.
- House bill H.R. 2608 extended the SBIR program until November 18, 2011.
- House bill H.R. 2112 extended the SBIR program again until December 16, 2011.
- The National Defense Authorization Act of 2012, Public Law 112–81, reauthorized the SBIR program until September 30, 2017.
- The National Defense Authorization Act of 2017, Public Law 114–328, reauthorized the SBIR program until September 30, 2022. Currently, the above program objective (3) from the 1982 Act is stated as: "[to] foster and encourage participation in innovation and entrepreneurship by women and socially or economically disadvantaged persons."[8]

The current set-aside amount is 3.2 percent of the extramural research budget of an agency, and the current award amounts are generally not more than $150,000 for a six-month Phase I award and generally not more than

$1,000,000 for a two-year Phase II award. Under certain conditions, an agency can increase Phase I and Phase II awards above these caps by up to 50 percent.

Arguably, the first formal statement of U.S. technology policy since the productivity slowdown in the 1970s and 1980s was set forth in *U.S. Technology Policy* (OSTP, 1990). Some may appropriately take issue with this statement arguing that a more appropriate and longer lasting formal statement of U.S. technology policy can be found in Vannevar Bush's *Science—the Endless Frontier* (1945). In fact, we have previously suggested that this is a reasonable point of view (see Link and Cunningham, 2021). Regardless, there are important statements in *U.S. Technology Policy* that are focused on the innovation-related importance of small firms. For example (OSTP, 1990, p. 2):

> The goal of U.S. technology policy is to make the best use of technology in achieving the national goals of improved quality of life for all Americans, continued economic growth, and national security.
>
> The goal of U.S. technology policy is to be achieved by maintaining a strong science and technology base, a healthy economic environment conducive to innovation and diffusion of new technologies, and by developing mutually beneficial international science and technology relationships. Implementation of the policy must recognize that all parts of the economy—the Federal Government, state and local governments, industry, and academia—have roles to play.
>
> [And] the Federal Government, industry, and academia need to take advantage of opportunities for: technology transfer and research cooperation, particularly involving *small* [emphasis added] and mid-sized companies …

Characteristic funding patterns associated with the SBIR program are described in the following section of this chapter in an effort to provide context about the program as well as about the unanticipated consequences associated with the program.

Patterns of SBIR Funding

Table 4.1 provides aggregate (i.e., across all SBIR funding agencies) data on a fiscal year by fiscal year basis on the number of Phase I SBIR awards awarded each year, the number of firms receiving Phase I awards, and the award or obligated amounts. These data cover the fiscal years (hereafter simply years) 1983 through 2019 and through part of 2020. The awarded/obligation amounts in the table are in current dollars.

Table 4.2 is constructed in a manner similar to Table 4.1 for Phase II awards. It should be noted that the first year of data in Table 4.1 corresponds to Phase I awards in 1983, one year following the passage of the 1982 Act. The first year of data on Phase II awards in Table 4.2 is 1984, the year following the first year of Phase 1 awards.

Table 4.1 *Phase I SBIR awards, by fiscal year*

Fiscal Year	Number of Awards	Number of Firms	Awarded/ *Obligated* Amount	Fiscal Year	Number of Awards	Number of Firms	Awarded/ *Obligated* Amount ($)
1983	785	543	37,849,979	2002	5112	2573	421,602,299
1984	1011	704	49,089,442	2003	5085	2716	466,036,528
1985	1472	961	73,896,275	2004	4654	2620	549,370,249
1986	1585	1018	81,208,028	2005	4401	2457	501,987,918
1987	2054	1224	103,101,073	2006	3942	2187	479,094,283
1988	1934	1202	97,925,372	2007	3845	2088	446,992,522
1989	2032	1249	102,062,893	2008	3734	2106	470,170,142
1990	2355	1377	119,935,774	2009	4091	2211	529,241,601
1991	2614	1474	131,619,712	2010	4362	2433	576,798,618
1992	2496	1411	125,446,032	2011	3628	2053	507,616,904
1993	2922	1627	159,223,042	2012	3417	1974	561,636,557
1994	3097	1815	220,340,738	2013	3016	1856	489,444,702
1995	3066	1764	234,502,269	2014	3088	1866	504,868,344
1996	2829	1671	227,502,449	2015	2808	1801	*486,397,153*
1997	3332	1900	277,947,434	2016	2960	1813	*486,428,076*
1998	2984	1736	258,538,921	2017	3217	1972	*568,183,152*
1999	3335	1931	290,552,147	2018	3135	2051	*600,691,501*
2000	3887	2135	290,089,114	2019	4001	2627	*700,496,994*
2001	4224	2193	303,728,836	2020	3915	2613	*669,512,568*

Source: Small Business Administration, https://www.sbir.gov/ (accessed October 21, 2020).
Note: Obligated award amounts are in italics. Awarded/*Obligated* amounts are in current dollars. According to the SBIR website—https://www.sbir.gov/analytics-dashboard (accessed May 11, 2021)—the Small Business Administration updates the figures in the table periodically.

Table 4.2 *Phase II SBIR awards, by fiscal year*

Fiscal Year	Number of Awards	Number of Firms	Awarded/*Obligated* Amount ($)	Fiscal Year	Number of Awards	Number of Firms	Awarded/*Obligated* Amount ($)
1983				2002	1587	1034	1,072,914,982
1984	275	219	99,865,866	2003	1734	1179	1,268,509,050
1985	349	288	118,508,595	2004	2076	1397	1,724,311,459
1986	567	417	221,327,680	2005	1933	1340	1,631,379,302
1987	688	522	165,126,726	2006	2032	1367	1,784,578,942
1988	704	500	291,102,873	2007	1613	1090	1,283,558,922
1989	749	564	291,400,429	2008	1893	1224	1,637,211,815
1990	834	595	327,631,206	2009	1836	1201	1,602,269,380
1991	748	575	317,061,989	2010	1944	1253	1,728,128,817
1992	909	652	391,770,868	2011	1870	1191	1,627,304,633
1993	1035	716	463,050,953	2012	1586	1066	1,486,042,334
1994	886	635	374,688,771	2013	1470	1009	1,442,928,259
1995	1255	914	713,452,816	2014	1481	1063	1,546,021,334
1996	1190	848	686,650,645	2015	1646	1139	*1,723,663,827*
1997	1407	975	844,359,394	2016	1650	1164	*1,824,237,403*
1998	1254	896	779,466,131	2017	1911	1272	*2,031,170,850*
1999	1238	880	816,280,030	2018	1703	1173	*2,133,179,742*
2000	1330	937	756,939,239	2019	2132	1441	*2,513,287,197*
2001	1524	1036	862,037,937	2020	2061	1542	*2,638,013,775*

Source: Small Business Administration, https://www.sbir.gov/ (accessed October 20, 2020).
Note: The first Phase I awards were in 1983 and thus the first Phase II awards were in 1984. Obligated award amounts are in italics. Awarded/*Obligated* amounts are in current dollars. According to the SBIR website—https://www.sbir.gov/analytics-dashboard (accessed May 11, 2021)—the Small Business Administration updates the figures in the table periodically.

It should also be noted that the total number of Phase II awards in a given year is less than the total number of Phase I awards in the previous year. For example, in 2013 the total number of Phase I awards was 3,016, but the total number of Phase II awards in 2014 was 1,481. Less than one-half of the Phase I funded research projects continued as Phase II funded research projects.

The pattern of Phase I and Phase II awards from Table 4.1 and Table 4.2 are illustrated in the following figures.

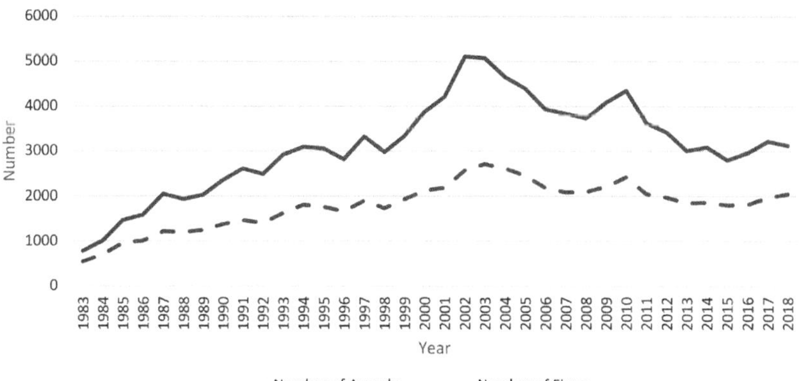

Source: Small Business Administration, https://www.sbir.gov/ (accessed October 20, 2020).

Figure 4.3 *Trend in number of Phase I SBIR awards and number of funded firms, by fiscal year*

Figure 4.3 shows the number of Phase I awards and the corresponding number of funded firms, by year. Figure 4.4 shows the same for Phase II awards. Since the peak in the early 2000s, both numbers in Figure 4.3 have declined. The related Figure 4.4 shows a slightly later in time peak in the number of Phase II awards and the number of Phase II funded firms, but the decline since the peak has been both milder and more sporadic.

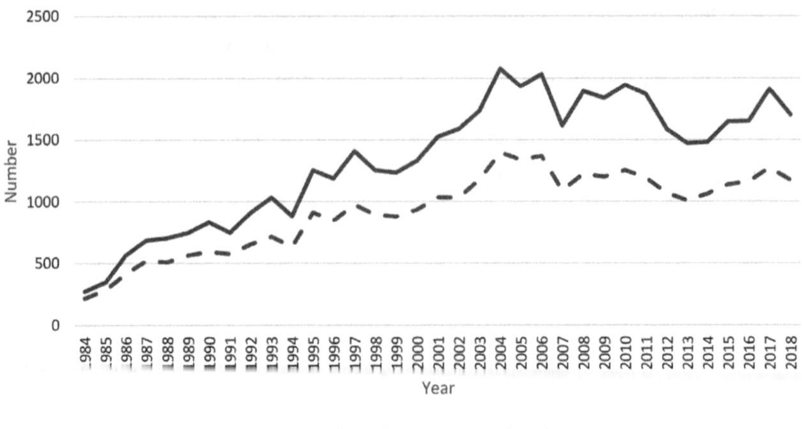

Source: Small Business Administration, https://www.sbir.gov/ (accessed October 20, 2020).

Figure 4.4 *Trend in number of Phase II SBIR awards and number of funded firms, by fiscal year*

The ratio of Phase II awards to Phase I awards, with a one-year lag, is shown in Figure 4.5 to have been around 40 percent until recently. Since about 2013, the ratio has generally been increasing.

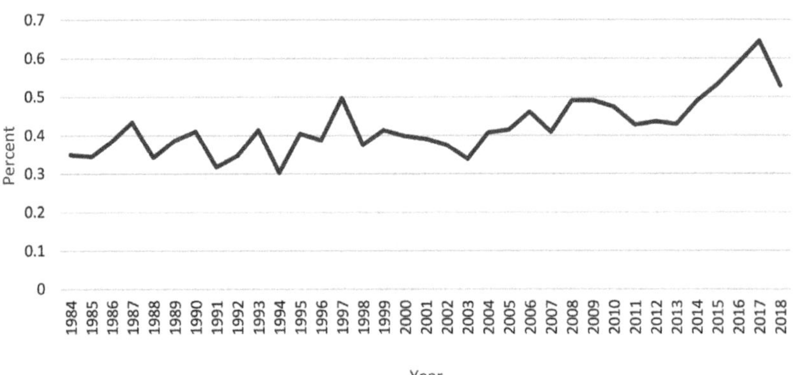

Figure 4.5 *Ratio of Phase II awards in year (t +1) to Phase I awards in year (t), by fiscal year*

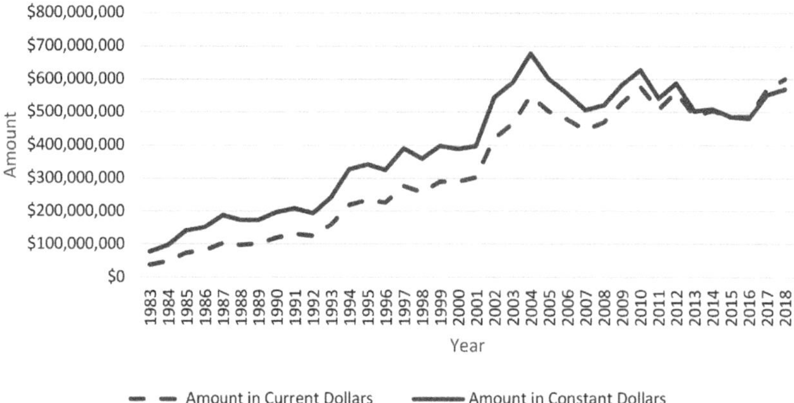

Source: Small Business Administration, https://www.sbir.gov/ (accessed October 20, 2020) and Federal Reserve Bank of St. Louis, https://fred.stlouisfed.org/series/USAGDPDEFAISMEI (accessed October 20, 2020).

Figure 4.6 *Trend in Phase I SBIR award amounts and obligated amounts for year 2015 forward, by fiscal year in current and constant $2015*

Figure 4.6 is a companion to Figure 4.3, and Figure 4.7 is a companion to Figure 4.4. Figure 4.6 shows the awarded/obligated amounts for Phase I in both current dollars (from Table 4.1) and in constant 2015 dollars. The GDP Implicit Price Deflator was used to convert the current dollar awarded/obligation amounts to constant dollar amounts with 2015 = 100. The important takeaway from both figures is that the amount of Phase I and Phase II awards/obligations has been increasing over time. This is of course due in part to that fact that the SBIR set-aside percentages have increased over time as have the maximum amounts allowed for a Phase I and Phase II award.

Table 4.3 *Cumulative number of Phase I SBIR awards and funded firms, by funding agency*

Agency	Number of Awards	Number of Firms	Awarded/*Obligated* Amount ($)
Department of Defense (DOD)	52,112	10,219	4,551,626,471
Department of Health and Human Services (HHS)	26,960	8,862	4,236,634,339
Department of Energy (DOE)	8,476	2,624	913,204,302
National Aeronautics and Space Administration (NASA)	10,556	2,985	837,100,214
National Science Foundation (NSF)	8,845	5,135	943,960,172
U.S. Department of Agriculture (USDA)	2,447	1,586	170,726,800
Department of Homeland Security (DHS)	675	436	73,049,948
Department of Education (ED)	967	578	62,780,363
Department of Commerce (DOC)	1064	732	73,483,978
Environmental Protection Agency (EPA)	1357	608	88,438,146
Department of Transportation (DOT)	770	531	63,165,877
Department of Interior (DOI)	15	15	485,280
Nuclear Regulatory Commission (NRC)	113	86	5,551,977

Source: Small Business Administration, https://www.sbir.gov/ (accessed October 20, 2020).
Note: Awarded and obligated amounts are in current dollars.

Table 4.3 disaggregates the above Phase I awarded/obligation funding information (see Table 4.1) by agency. Cumulative award numbers as well as funded firm numbers, and awarded/obligated dollar amounts, are shown in the table. Clearly, the Department of Defense (DOD) is the largest participant in the SBIR program in terms of number of awards as well as funding dollars. The Department of Health and Human Services (HHS) ranks a close second in terms of funding amounts, but a distant second in terms of number of awards. The average amount of each HHS Phase I award is thus greater than the average amount of each DOD Phase I award.

Table 4.4 (see Table 4.2) is the Phase II companion to Table 4.3. Again, DOD ranks highest in terms of number of awards, number of funded firms, and awarded/obligated amounts, followed by HHS.

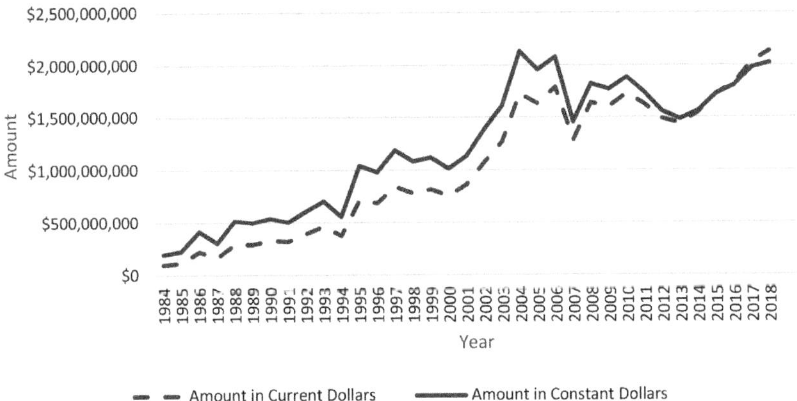

Source: Small Business Administration, https://www.sbir.gov/ (accessed October 20, 2020) and Federal Reserve Bank of St. Louis, https://fred.stlouisfed.org/series/USAGDPDEFAISMEI (accessed October 20, 2020).

Figure 4.7 *Trend in Phase II SBIR award amounts and obligated amounts for year 2015 forward, by fiscal year in current and constant $2015*

Table 4.4 *Cumulative number of Phase II SBIR awards and funded firms, by funding agency*

Agency	Number of Awards	Number of Firms	Awarded/*Obligated* Amount ($)
Department of Defense (DOD)	24,185	5,895	18,728,728,772
Department of Health and Human Services (HHS)	9,742	4,134	9,527,765,347
Department of Energy (DOE)	3,606	1,376	2,883,792,543
National Aeronautics and Space Administration (NASA)	4,382	1,647	2,622,473,760
National Science Foundation (NSF)	2,847	2,064	1,523,006,528
U.S. Department of Agriculture (USDA)	964	708	310,595,702
Department of Homeland Security (DHS)	349	206	273,102,362
Department of Education (ED)	319	204	142,014,752
Department of Commerce (DOC)	464	363	126,330,315
Environmental Protection Agency (EPA)	462	228	104,579,716
Department of Transportation (DOT)	322	230	14 ,060,939
Department of Interior (DOI)	0	0	0
Nuclear Regulatory Commission (NRC)	55	43	9,147,195

Source: Small Business Administration, https://www.sbir.gov/ (accessed October 20, 2020).
Note: Awarded and obligated amounts are in current dollars.

Figure 4.8 shows the ratio of the number of Phase II awards to the number of Phase I awards without accounting for any lag period. The data in Figure 4.8 are based on the cumulative agency numbers in Tables 4.3 and 4.4. As in Figure 4.5, the ratio across agencies is about 40 percent.

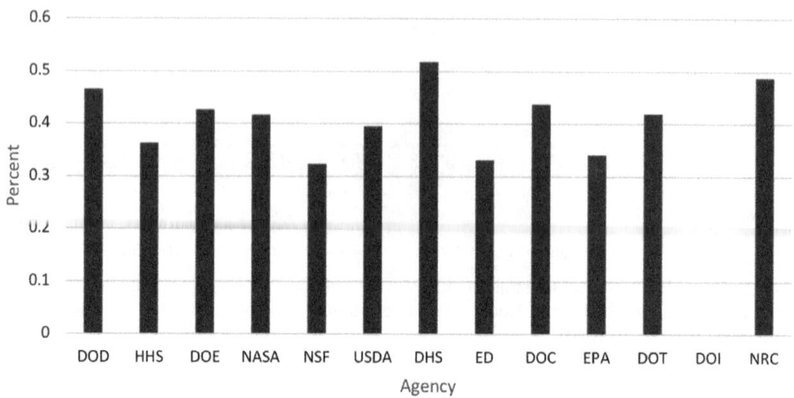

Source: Small Business Administration, https://www.sbir.gov/ (accessed October 20, 2020).
Key:
DOD (Department of Defense)
HHS (Department of Health and Human Services)
DOE (Department of Energy)
NASA National Aeronautics and Space Administration)
NSF (National Science Foundation)
USDA (U.S. Department of Agriculture)
DHS (Department of Homeland Security)
ED (Department of Education)
DOC (Department of Commerce)
EPA (Environmental Protection Agency)
DOT (Department of Transportation)
DOI (Department of Interior)
NRC (Nuclear Regulatory Commission)

Figure 4.8 *Ratio of cumulative Phase II awards to cumulative Phase I awards, by funding agency*

Figures 4.9 and 4.10 focus specifically on DOD. The trend on Phase I awarded/obligation amounts in both current and constant collars is increasing until the early 2000s. The same is true for Phase II awarded/obligated amounts.

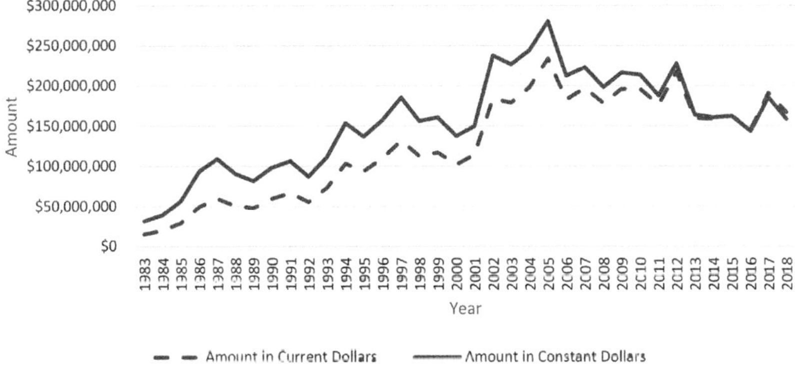

Source: Small Business Administration, https://www.sbir.gov/ (accessed October 20, 2020) and Federal Reserve Bank of St. Louis, https://fred.stlouisfed.org/series/USAGDPDEFAISMEI(accessed October 20, 2020).

Figure 4.9 *Trend in Department of Defense Phase I SBIR award amounts and obligated amounts, by fiscal year in current and constant $2015*

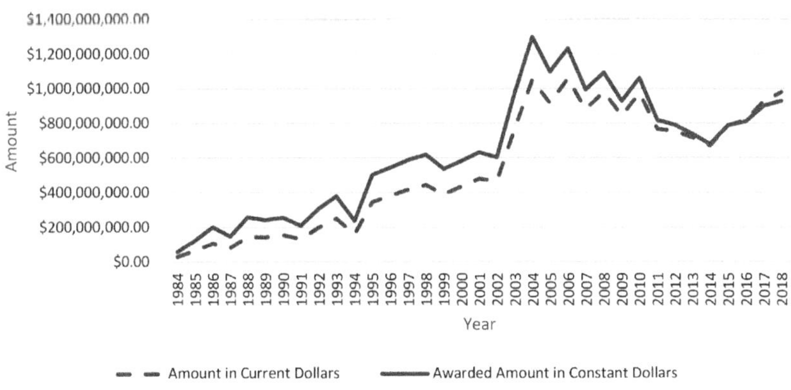

Source: Small Business Administration, https://www.sbir.gov/ (accessed October 20, 2020) and Federal Reserve Bank of St. Louis, https://fred.stlouisfed.org/series/USAGDPDEFAISMEI (accessed October 20, 2020).

Figure 4.10 *Trend in Department of Defense Phase II SBIR award amounts and obligated amounts, by fiscal year in current and constant $2015*

Figures 4.11 and 4.12 correspond to HHS. Phase I award amounts increased until the early 2000s as did Phase II award amounts with a lag, but afterwards the trend in Phase I awarded/obligation amounts is more sporadic than is the trend in Phase II awarded/obligation amounts except for the visible dip in 2007.

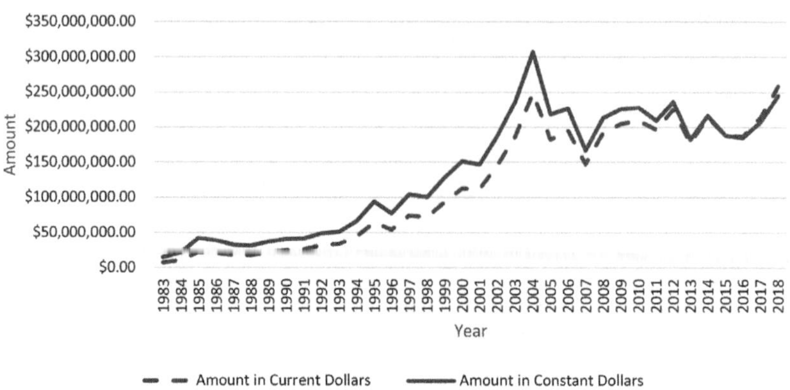

Source: Small Business Administration, https://www.sbir.gov/ (accessed October 20, 2020) and Federal Reserve Bank of St. Louis, https://fred.stlouisfed.org/series/USAGDPDEFAISMEI (accessed October 20, 2020).

Figure 4.11 *Trend in Department of Health and Human Services Phase I SBIR award amounts and obligated amounts, by fiscal year in current and constant $2015*

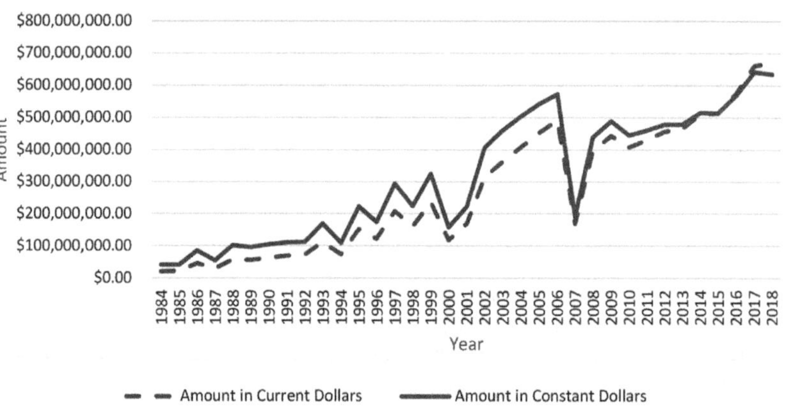

Source: Small Business Administration, https://www.sbir.gov/ (accessed October 20, 2020) and Federal Reserve Bank of St. Louis, https://fred.stlouisfed.org/series/USAGDPDEFAISMEI (accessed October 20, 2020).

Figure 4.12 *Trend in Department of Health and Human Services Phase II SBIR award amounts and obligated amounts, by fiscal year in current and constant $2015*

Table 4.5 shows the allocation of 2014 Phase II award amounts for DOD, the National Institutes of Health (NIH) within HHS, the Department of Energy (DOE), the National Aeronautics and Space Administration (NASA), and the NSF.[9] DOD ranks first followed by NIH. Together these two agencies accounted for more than 50 percent of Phase II funding in 2014.

Table 4.5 Distribution of Year 2014 Phase II awards, by SBIR funding agency

Agency	Percent of Award Amount (rounded) (%)
DOD	43.4
NIH	15.1
DOE	9.2
NASA	6.7
NSF	4.9
All Others	20.8

Source: Small Business Administration, https://www.sbir.gov/ (accessed October 20, 2020)
Key:
DOD (Department of Defense)
NIH (National Institutes of Health)
DOE (Department of Energy)
NASA (National Aeronautics and Space Administration)
NSF (National Science Foundation)

Unanticipated Consequences: The Sale of SBIR Funded Technology

In anticipation of the scheduled 2008 reauthorization of the SBIR program, the U.S. Congress entered into an agreement with the National Academies for the National Research Council to conduct a comprehensive study of how the SBIR program has stimulated technological innovation and used small businesses to meet Federal research and development needs.[10]

The National Research Council concluded its study of the SBIR programs in the DOD, NIH, DOE, NASA, and the NSF in 2008. And, the Council's five agencies focused reports to Congress were important in the reauthorization of the program. The five agencies considered in the National Research Council study represented 97 percent of all Phase II projects funded by the 11 agencies that participated in the SBIR program in 2005, the year of the study's data collection survey.

An inspection of the survey data collected by the National Research Council in 2005 from a randomly selected set of completed Phase II projects might suggest that one of the results from Federal funding of small firms was not being anticipated.

Consider the following. Of the 11,214 Phase II projects funded by the five agencies studied by the National Research Council, a random sample of 1,878 firms were surveyed in 2005, and the information discussed below was provided by a responding sample of 1,279 (11.41 percent of the population) firms. This sample focused on Phase II projects that were funded over the years 1992 through 2001. The firms in this sample of Phase II projects responded to the focal survey question: Did you sell the rights to the technology developed during this Phase II SBIR funded project to a foreign firm or investor?[11]

Fifteen of the firms responding to the National Research Council survey responded that they had, at the time of the 2005 survey, finalized the sale of the rights to the technology developed from their U.S. taxpayer funded Phase II SBIR funded project to a foreign firm or investor. Another 31 of the firms responding to the survey reported that they were involved in ongoing negotiations with a foreign firm or investor for the rights to their SBIR funded and thus developed technology.

In 2019 dollars, the amount of the Phase II SBIR awards invested in the development of the 15 technologies sold to foreign firms or investors totaled $13.52 million; and the amount of the Phase II SBIR awards invested in the development of the 31 technologies being negotiated for sale to foreign firms or investors totaled $26.74 million. If all of these negotiations were finalized, and if one extrapolates from the sample of 1,279 Phase II projects to the population of all 11,214 funded Phase II projects, as much as $353 million in SBIR funded technology is either no longer available to U.S. agencies to enhance the nation's competitiveness in international markets, or if available, it is available at an additional cost to taxpayers because of the transfer of ownership of the technology. And, if one considers this same scenario for Phase II projects funded beyond the 1992 through 2011 time period, the $353 million amount would be larger.

In all likelihood, the sale of SBIR funded technology to foreign firms or investors was a profit-maximizing strategy by the firms involved. However, a relevant question is: Was that profit-maximizing strategy in line with the anticipated behavior of SBIR funded companies by policy makers when the program was started and when the program was continually reauthorized by Congress? Our reading of the underlying legislation is that the relevant policy makers anticipated that Phase II technologies funded through U.S. taxpayers' dollars would reside within the United States for the benefit of the U.S. agencies that funded the research.

Nowhere in the enabling legislation are constraints placed on funded companies about their developed technologies other than the policy goal of commercialization of the technology. If policy makers believe that the commercialization ownership of publicly funded technologies developed for U.S. agencies by U.S. firms should reside in those U.S. firms and U.S. agencies, then perhaps policy makers will react to $353 million or more of technology sold to foreign firms and investors as an unanticipated consequence from current legislation and thus offer policy remedies.

CONCLUDING OBSERVATIONS

With any technology policy or innovation policy, unanticipated consequences are part of the implementation process. Legislators and policy makers in developing policy in this arena have to make assumptions based on available data and their engagement with stakeholders. The policy challenge is ensuring that the designed policy instrument is chosen correctly and targeted appropriately to support behavioral changes among decision makers within targeted firms. For technology policies and innovation policies to be effective, legislators and policy makers need to consider how they will influence the end user/policy recipient. The fear of unanticipated consequences should not lead to policy paralysis in this arena, where legislators or policy makers pursue no substantive technology policy or innovation policy to avoid making a mistake. On the contrary, policy makers should be experimental in their policy responses, and legislators need to be more open to supporting a portfolio of creative policy responses. Leyden and Link (2015) refer to such response creativity by the term *public sector entrepreneurship*. The demands emanating from the need for technology policies and innovation policies require responsive, lean, and effective initiatives that can support appropriate hurdle rates for private-sector firms and for society. The timing of such hurdle rates may not neatly align to election cycles or may be realized over long time periods. For situations with negative unanticipated consequences, swift responses from policy makers and legislators are required.

NOTES

1. Unanticipated consequences associated with a legislated policy are not necessarily at odds with the concept of government failure (Dolfsma, 2011; Le Grand, 1991; Wolf, 1988). One might think of government failure as purposeful public-sector involvement in a market economy that results in the market economy being less efficient than before the public sector's involvement. Dolfsma (2011, p. 597) wrote: "The non-exhaustive list of four different ways in which government can fail will draw mostly on scholarly work in the philosophy of law. When formulating rules, then, government can be (1) too specific, (2) too broad, (3) arbitrary, or (4) setting out rules that conflict with other rules it has set out to address other, related (possibly primarily non-economic) issues possibly for the same practice." Dolfsma's view, which draws on the literature on government failure—Wolf's (1988) writings in particular—is that government failure results from ill-formed rules (i.e., ill-formed policies that set forth guidelines).

2. Merton (1936, p. 894) also wrote: "In some one of its numerous forms, the problem of the unanticipated consequences of purposive action has been treated by virtually every substantial contributor to the long history of social thought. Some of the modern theorists, though their contributions are by no means of equal importance, are: Machiavelli, Vico, Adam Smith (and some later classical economists), Marx, Engels, Wundt, Pareto, Max Weber, Graham Wallas, Cooley, Sorokin, Gini, Chapin, von Schelting."
3. This statement assumes that all resources have alternative uses.
4. This section draws directly from Leyden and Link (2015) and Link and Cunningham (2021).
5. Roland Tibbetts, a Senior Program Officer at NSF, understood as early as 1972 the importance of small technology-based firms, and thus he allocated funds in their direction. Tibbetts's efforts led to the establishment of a program in 1977 that would be the precursor to the SBIR program. See https://www.sbir.gov/tutorials/program-basics/tutorial-5 (accessed October 21, 2020).
6. We have written about the SBIR program many times. Thus, duplication of text and emphasis is unavoidable. See, for examples, Leyden and Link (2015), Link and Cunningham (2021), Link and Scott (2012), and a collection of authored and co-authored writings in Link (2013).
7. It has been argued that the SBIR program is an example of public-sector entrepreneurship (see Hayter et al., 2018; Leyden and Link, 2015). Leyden and Link (2015, p. 46) define the concept of public-sector entrepreneurship in the following way: "Public sector entrepreneurship … refers to innovative public policy initiatives that generate greater economic prosperity by transforming a status quo economic environment into one that is more conducive to economic units engaging in creative activities in the face of uncertainty." Leyden and Link (2015) go on to make a case that the passage of the 1982 Act is an example of public-sector entrepreneurship. The 1982 Act redirects property rights that bring about the transfer of existing knowledge from a university to the private sector for commercial exploitation.
8. See https://www.sbir.gov/about/about-sbir (accessed October 21, 2020).
9. Fiscal year 2014 was chosen for Table 4.5 because it is the most recent year of actual award amounts. Beginning in 2015, only obligated award amount information is available.
10. See http://www.nasonline.org/about-nas/history/archives/milestones-in-NAS-history/organization-of-the-nrc.html (accessed October 21, 2020).
11. The actual question on the National Research Council survey was: "As a result of the technology developed during this [Phase II] project, which of the following describes your firm's activities with other firms and investors?" The activities listed on the survey included Licensing Agreement(s), Sale of company, Partial sale of company, Sale of technology rights, Company merger, Joint venture agreement, Marketing/distribution agreement(s), Manufacturing agreement(s), R&D agreement(s), and Customer alliance(s). Our assumption is the sale of technology rights is an unanticipated consequence from the SBIR program.

5. The technology policy environment

INTRODUCTION

The theme of Chapter 2 is that private-sector R&D is the target variable for technology policy. Policy efforts to increase private-sector investments in R&D through tax incentives or through direct subsidies will stimulate the development of additional technology; and that new technology leads to new innovations entering the market, enhanced productivity growth, and eventually enhanced economic growth. We emphasized these relationships in our framework diagram, which is discussed below, and in our overall behavior paradigm:

$$R\&D \rightarrow technology \rightarrow innovation \rightarrow economic\ growth$$

In this chapter, we focus on the shaded cell in our framework diagram, reproduced here as Figure 5.1, "Technology policy environment."

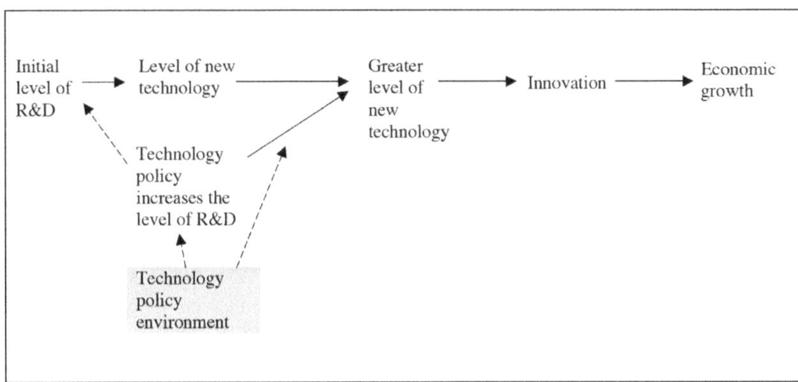

Source: Prepared by the authors.

Figure 5.1 *Framework for explaining the role of investments in R&D and the role of technology policy and innovation policy in the economy*

We define two elements of the technology policy environment that leverage the amount of private-sector investments in R&D and the impact that private-sector investments in R&D have on technology development and thus innovation. These elements, which are present in all countries to varying degrees, are an operational patent system and an environment supportive for firms engaging in collaborative R&D.[1]

We discuss patent systems in the next section of this chapter followed by a discussion of the collaborative R&D environment. We will expand on these ideas in Chapter 8; there we introduce the "Technology policy ecosystem" into our framework.

PATENT SYSTEMS

A Brief History of Patent Systems

The origin of patent systems, industrial patent systems in particular, traces to the Italians. Filippo Brunelleschi began to build the cupola of the cathedral of Florence in 1419 (Frumkin, 1945, p. 144):[2,3]

> In 1421 the State of Florence granted [Brunelleschi] an exclusive right, valid for three years, to build and use a device of his invention for transporting heavy loads on the Arno and other rivers, and it was even stipulated that the work of anybody imitating his invention should be burned.

And, in 1449, John of Utynam, a Flemish glassmaker (Kwong, 2014):

> … is considered the first person on record to have been awarded an English patent. Granted by King Henry VI, the exclusive rights gave John a 20-year monopoly on producing stained glass—a technique that was until that point unknown in England.

Moving ahead in time, in 1624, the British Parliament enacted the Statute of Monopolies (Khan, undated):[4]

> [It] repealed the practice of royal monopoly grants to all except patentees of inventions. The Statute of Monopolies allowed patent rights of fourteen years for 'the sole making or working of any manner of new manufacture within this realm to the first and true inventor …'

Building on the British activities in this intellectual property protection arena, the United States, in Article 1, Section 8, of the U.S. Constitution (1787), set forth the foundation for the U.S. patent system. As stated in Article 1:

> The Congress shall have power to … promote the Progress of Science and useful Arts, by securing for limited Times to Authors and Inventors the exclusive Right to their respective Writings and Discoveries …

And, soon thereafter, the Patent Act was enacted in the United States in 1790:

> *Be it enacted by the Senate and House of Representatives of the United States of America in Congress assembled,* That upon the petition of any person or persons to the Secretary of State, the Secretary for the department of war, and the Attorney General of the United States, setting forth, that he, she, or they, hath or have invented or discovered any useful art, manufacture, engine, machine, or device, or any improvement therein not before known or used, and praying that a patent may be granted therefor, it shall and may be lawful to … deem the invention or discovery sufficiently useful and important, to cause letters patent to be made out in the name of the United States … and thereupon granting to such petitioner or petitioners, his, her or their heirs, administrators or assigns for any term not exceeding fourteen years, the sole and exclusive right and liberty of making, constructing, using and vending to others to be used, the said invention or discovery …

From a European perspective, the European Patent Office (EPO) is the main focus of patent activity across Europe. The EPO dates to the signing of the European Patent Convention in Munich, Germany, on October 5, 1973 when 16 countries signed this treaty that established the basis for the European patent system. This European Patent Convention's 178 articles covered such matters as the organizational structures of the EPO, the Administrative Council, patent law, requirements for filing a patent, patent appeals as well as common and general provisions. The opening articles stated the founding principles of the European patent system:[5]

> Article 1: *European law for the grant of patents*
> A system of law, common to the Contracting States, for the grant of patents for invention is established by the Convention.
>
> Article 2: *European patent*
> (1) Patent granted under this Convention shall be called European patents.
> (2) The European patent shall, in each of the Contracting States for which it is granted, have the effect of and be subject to the same conditions as a national patent granted by that State, unless this Convention provides otherwise.
>
> Article 3: *Territorial effect*
> The grant of a European patent may be requested for one or more of the Contracting States.

Article 4: *European Patent Organisation*

(1) A European Patent Organisation, thereinafter referred to as the Organisation, is established by this Convention. It shall have administrative and financial autonomy.

(2) The organs of the Organisation shall be
   (a) the European Patent Office;
   (b) the Administrative Council;

(3) The task of the Organisation shall be to grant European patents. This shall be carried out by the European Patent Office supervised by the Administrative Council

One of the objectives of the European Patent Convention and the creation of the EPO was to make it attractive and efficient (e.g., time and fees) for firms and individuals to apply for patents. Moreover, the EPO and the patent regime were designed to be attractive because patents apply to all countries that have signed up to this Convention negating the need for individual country patent applications. By 1988, the EPO had granted its 100,000th patent and the number reached 200,000 patents granted in 1992. By 2019, 181,406 patent applications were received by the EPO compared to 160,004 in 2015. Huawei, Samsung, United Technologies, and Siemens were the top applicant companies in 2019, with some 45 percent of patent applications coming from European companies and another 35 percent coming from U.S. companies (see EPO, 2020a, 2020b).

The Economics of Patents

Figure 5.2 illustrates what we call a model for the economics of a patent system from the perspective of a private-sector firm. On the vertical axis is the marginal private rate of return to R&D, and on the horizontal axis is the level of investments in R&D. As previously discussed, the marginal private rate of return schedules are downward sloping reflecting diminishing returns to R&D in any given time period, and for simplicity we assume the marginal private rate of return schedule to be linear, at least linear over relevant levels of investments in R&D.

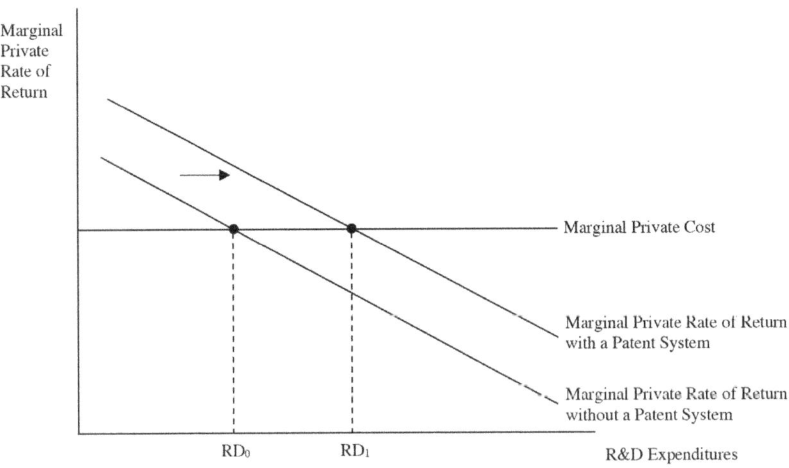

Source: Based on Link (2006).

Figure 5.2 *The economics of a patent system*

One of the two marginal private rate of return schedules in the figure represents private-sector firm investments in R&D in the absence of an available patent system (i.e., either a patent system specific to the country in which the firm operates or an international patent system), and the other marginal private rate of return schedule represents private-sector firm investments in R&D with an available patent system. The firm will determine its profit-maximizing level of R&D spending where the marginal private cost of R&D, conceptualized as the opportunity cost of R&D investments, equals the marginal private rate of return from R&D. As illustrated, the firm will choose to invest at the level of R&D shown to be RD_0.

A firm that receives a patent for its R&D-based technology—which grants the firm monopoly privilege for a legislated period of years, generally 20 years—will realize an increase in its marginal private rate of return from its investments in R&D, thus shifting the marginal private rate of return schedule upward and to the right in Figure 5.2 as indicated by the horizontal arrow. At all levels of R&D, the marginal rate of return is higher with a patent system than without one. The intersection of the new marginal private rate of return schedule and the marginal private cost schedule defines the new optimal R&D investment level for the firm; it is RD_1.[6]

In other words, the economics of a patent system is that it provides, through an intellectual property protection mechanism, a financial incentive (i.e., a higher rate of return) for firms to increase their level of investments in R&D.

Firms use patents as one of the means to enhance their competitive position and to choose a corporate strategy (see Cunningham and Harney, 2012). Patents can be integrated into a new product or service that a firm brings into the market. Firms can also use patents to enhance their existing operational efficiency or their existing product or service offering. Typically, the primary organizational responsibility of utilizing patents tends to lie with new product developments teams within an R&D unit or function of the firm.

While the framework in Figure 5.1 relates to patent systems as an element of the technology policy environment, it is important to emphasize that even with a patent system a private-sector firm might use other intellectual property protection mechanisms, either exclusively or as part of a patent protection portfolio. For example, the academic literature shows that larger firms tend to patent more frequently than smaller firms especially small entrepreneurial firms. Also, those firms that use a portfolio of formal intellectual property protection mechanisms (patents, trademarks, and copyrights) are mostly in the high-technology sector (see Link and Van Hasselt, 2020).

Many empirical studies illustrate that patents positively influence firms' performance (see Artz et al., 2003; Belenzon and Patacconi, 2014; Brouwer and Kleinknecht, 1999; Mazzoleni and Nelson, 1998; Smyth et al., 1972; Tsai, 2005). For example, Andries and Faems (2013) studied manufacturing firms, and they concluded that patents supported their innovation performance, enhancing their profit margins, and enhanced their ability to exploit their knowledge base. Similarly, a study of more than 200 U.K. firms from 1968 affirms that patents significantly improved their market value and productivity (see Bloom and Van Reenen, 2002). In a large-scale U.S. study using patent and economic census data, Balasubramanian and Sivadasan (2011) found that firms also increased their skill, capital, scope, and size from patenting. Given rapid technological changes, firms can use patenting for strategic purposes or what Artz et al. (2010, p. 725) term *patents as strategic weapons*. Hall and Ziedonis (2001), in their study of the U.S. semiconductor industry over the years 1979 to 1995, noted that some firms purposely built up their patent portfolios (to act as strategic weapons).[7]

Intensity of Patenting

Figure 5.3 shows the number of patent applications to the EPO by inventors—and inventors need not necessarily be in private-sector firms—in the United Kingdom and in the United States. Figure 5.4 shows the number of patent applications to the U.S. Patent and Trademark Office (USPTO) by inventors in the United Kingdom and in the United States.

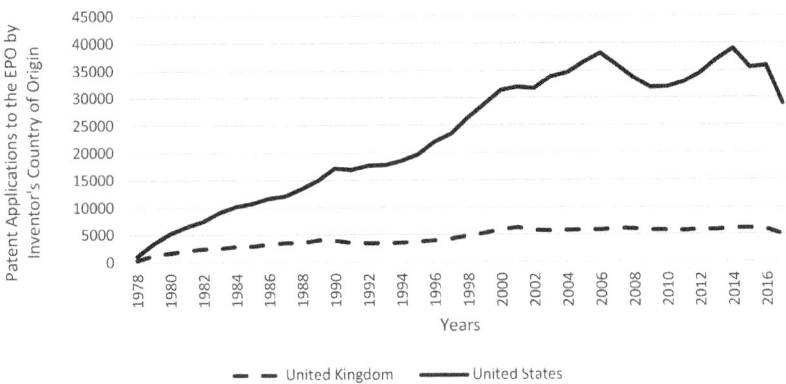

Source: https://stats.oecd.org/Index.aspx?DataSetCode=MSTI_PUB# (accessed May 10, 2020).

Figure 5.3 *Patent applications by United Kingdom and United States inventors to the European Patent Office (EPO) by inventor's country of residence, years 1978–2017*

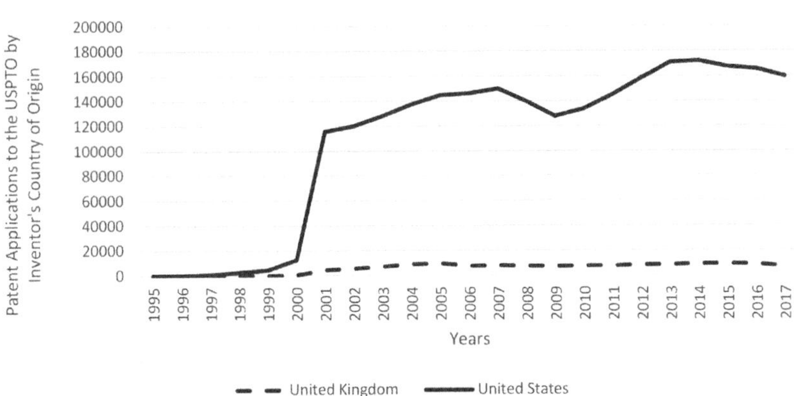

Source: https://stats.oecd.org/Index.aspx?DataSetCode=MSTI_PUB# (accessed May 10, 2020).

Figure 5.4 *Patent applications by United Kingdom and United States inventors to the U.S. Patent and Trademark Office (USPTO) by inventor's country of residence, years 1995–2017*

Table 5.1 *Patent applications to the European Patent Office and the U.S. Patent and Trademark Office by inventor's country of residence, year 2017*

Country	Applications to the EPO	Applications to the USPTO
Australia	749.9	1,840.2
Austria	1,883.1	1,282.7
Belgium	1,491.6	1,198.1
Canada	1,551.4	7,443.6
Chile	25.3	44.9
Colombia	9.1	34.4
Czech Republic	217.9	308.9
Denmark	1,144.9	969.7
Estonia	39.9	39.0
Finland	1,030.0	1,077.6
France	7,568.7	5,341.7
Germany	19,657.7	15,597.0
Greece	92.9	123.9
Hungary	130.0	125.9
Iceland	22.7	51.6
Ireland	330.6	877.6
Israel	1,154.3	4,473.6
Italy	4,007.4	2,726.1
Japan	15,519.1	49,108.4
Korea	5,620.7	19,602.2
Latvia	8.9	12.0
Lithuania	20.7	15.9
Luxembourg	90.1	46.8
Mexico	60.5	379.6
Netherlands	3,539.3	2,251.9
New Zealand	113.6	299.2
Norway	449.1	585.7
Poland	516.0	347.1
Portugal	172.3	175.0
Slovak Republic	55.6	46.9
Slovenia	128.6	43.8
Spain	1,357.6	841.6
Sweden	2,070.3	2,216.6

Country	Applications to the EPO	Applications to the USPTO
Switzerland	3,058.1	2,619.4
Turkey	698.7	163.3
United Kingdom	4,884.3	6,753.3
United States	28,928.6	159,399.7

Source: https://stats.oecd.org/Index.aspx?DataSetCode=MSTI_PUB# (accessed May 10, 2020).
Note: The data accounts for fractional counts.

Two patterns are evident from Figures 5.3 and 5.4. First, inventors from the United States often apply for patents at both the EPO and at the USPTO to a greater extent than do inventors from the United Kingdom, but population size is not controlled for in the figures. Second, patent applications vary to a greater extent in the United States year by year than they do in the United Kingdom.

Table 5.1 shows, for 2017, the number of patent applications to the EPO and to the USPTO, by country and by inventor's country of residence. The United States tops the list.

Table 5.2 *European Patent Office granted patents, top ten countries for years 2018 and 2019*

Rank	Country Origin	2019	2018	Change (%)
1	United States	34,614	31,136	11.2
2	Japan	22,423	21,343	5.1
3	Germany	21,198	20,804	1.9
4	France	8,800	8,610	2.2
5	Republic of Korea	7,247	6,262	15.7
6	People's Republic of China	6,229	4,831	28.9
7	Switzerland	4,770	4,452	7.1
8	Netherlands	4,326	3,782	14.4
9	United Kingdom	4,119	3,827	7.6
10	Sweden	3,838	3,537	8.5

Source: https://www.epo.org/about-us/annual-reports-statistics/statistics.html (accessed November 2, 2020).
Notes:
The analysis in the table is based on published patents granted by the EPO.
Country of origin is based on the country of residence of the first patentee listed on the published patent.
In cases where several patentees are mentioned on the published patent, the country of residence of the first patentee listed applies.

Table 5.2 shows, for years 2018 and 2019, the top patent granting countries by the EPO. Table 5.2 also shows for all of the top ten countries their year on year growth of patents being granted. Firms in the digital communication, medical technology, computer technology, electrical machinery apparatus, energy, and transport comprised the top five technology fields for patent application filed in year 2019 (EPO, 2020b, p. 4). About 72 percent of patent applications from European countries in 2019 came from large firms, university, and private research organizations (PROs). About 60 percent of the remaining 18 percent is accounted for by small and medium sized enterprises (i.e., firms) (SMEs) and individual inventors.

R&D COLLABORATIONS

To further enhance their competitive position, firms can pursue R&D collaborations with suppliers, competitors, universities, public research organizations, and firms in other industries and sectors (see Link, 2020a; Un and Asakawa, 2015). At the firm level, R&D collaboration decisions are intertwined with both the nature of the competitive environment and the innovation strategy that is being pursued (see Cunningham and Walsh, 2019). For example, firms may be pursuing open innovation strategies rather than closed. This, in turn, can mean some changes in the way in which R&D collaborations are selected and evaluated, particularly with respect to knowledge sharing and intellectual property management (see Bogers, 2011).

Firms' collaboration in R&D projects is intended to achieve several strategic goals.[8] Collaboration in R&D projects reduces redundancy because partners can distribute aspects of the research process (i.e., research activities as well as research costs) among themselves and then internally share their findings. As a result of sharing research information, collaboration in R&D thus reduces the per-project and per-partner cost of R&D, and through R&D collaboration, the time to reach research objectives is shortened.

Increasingly, universities and firms are pursuing R&D collaborations. The cost of R&D is a motivating factor for universities to engage in such collaborations (see Cohen et al., 1997; Link 2020a; Link and Wessner, 2011). Firms benefit through firm with university R&D collaborations by increased productivity, sharing of costs, and access to proprietary knowledge (see Cunningham and Link, 2015). R&D collaborations also enhance the economics of their technology scope (see Leyden and Link, 2015). Firm collaborations with industry, meaning firm collaborations with other industrial firms, benefit members of the collaborative venture in terms of technology recombination; research shows that these benefits differ based on the age of the firm (see Soh and Subramanian, 2014).[9] Firms also gain access to working with the scientists and their research teams. Such R&D collaborative arrangements may be formalized through publicly funded research grants through which the university's or PRO's scientists are the principal investigators (PIs) leading the funded project research program (see Cunningham et al., 2016; Cunningham et al., 2020; Mangematin et al., 2014). For SMEs, personal relationships and asset scarcity are factors that enhance such collaborations in terms of technology transfers (see O'Reilly and Cunningham, 2017). A further consideration for firms is the wider policy environment and the types of incentives that are available to support R&D collaborations (see Cunningham and Link, 2016). In such R&D collaborations, universities and industrial firms will use different key performance indicators throughout the life cycle of collaboration in R&D (see Albats et al., 2018).

Firm with university R&D collaborations can be formal arrangements through collaboration mechanisms such as joint research programs, consulting agreements, and contracts. There also may be informal ongoing contacts between individual researchers and research teams in multinational corporations (MNCs) as well as in SMEs. Based on a study of German manufacturing firms by Goel et al. (2017), the authors concluded that industrial scientists typically initiate collaborations with firms. The authors also concluded that scientists have more challenges collaborating with large firms than with small firms.[10] Cunningham et al. (2016), in a study of PIs, found that one of the barriers they experienced in such collaborations with industry was dealing with their organization hierarchy and power structures. To overcome such collaborative challenges, Starbuck (2001) suggested that firms need to manage such collaborations by ensuring that they are internally aligned with existing organization practices and norms.

To encourage greater university with industry R&D collaborations, governments use a range of policy interventions. One of the main interventions is the funding of basic and applied research programs that are led and managed by national funding agencies. For example, in a small country context, Science Foundation Ireland developed different research funding schemes that are designed to deliver science discovery and build collaborations with industry. Some of these interventions involved the creation of dedicated research centers in sectors that are of national importance to the Irish economy such as medical devices (see Barry, 2007; Grimes and Collins, 2009; Hilliard and Green, 2005). In the United Kingdom, Innovate UK and other funding bodies fund Knowledge Transfer Partnerships (KTPs) that are designed specifically to support university with firm R&D cooperation in commercialization. KTPs are designed to transfer knowledge that addresses a specific firm's needs (see Gertner et al., 2011), especially needs that involve co-creation of value (see Jones and Coates, 2020). The EU funds European Structural Programs across sectors that are designed in a manner to enhance the collaboration between firms and other stakeholders, such as enterprise support agencies, that explore and exploit new knowledge creation.

It is often the case that the membership of a collaborative research partnership involves both firms that compete in the market for similar technologies and firms that are involved in the supply chain associated with those technologies. It follows, then, that for firms to undertake collaborative research, the research will be toward the basic research end of the R&D spectrum rather than toward the development end of the R&D spectrum. Basic research results in per se knowledge, that is, knowledge that is not appropriable or knowledge that is a pure public good. Thus, the sharing of such knowledge will not necessarily give one firm a competitive advantage over another firm. However, firms have different motives for undertaking and seeking out R&D collaborations (see Arvanitis, 2012) such as the complexity of their being-developed technology as well as acquiring other competencies (see Bayona et al., 2001; Mothe and Quélin, 2000). Firm motivations can vary depending on the public funding instrument available such as through the European Framework Programmes (see Bach et al., 2014).

The economics of R&D collaboration is shown in Figure 5.5. The profit-maximizing firm will invest RD_0 in R&D. This level of investment is determined when the marginal private cost of conducting R&D, conceptualized as the opportunity cost of R&D investments, equals the marginal private rate of return from that specific R&D. As a result of research collaboration, the marginal private cost of R&D will decrease due to decreased redundancy and a shorter research time, and thus the firm will, in a profit-maximizing manner, increase its investments in R&D from RD_0 to RD_1 as drawn.

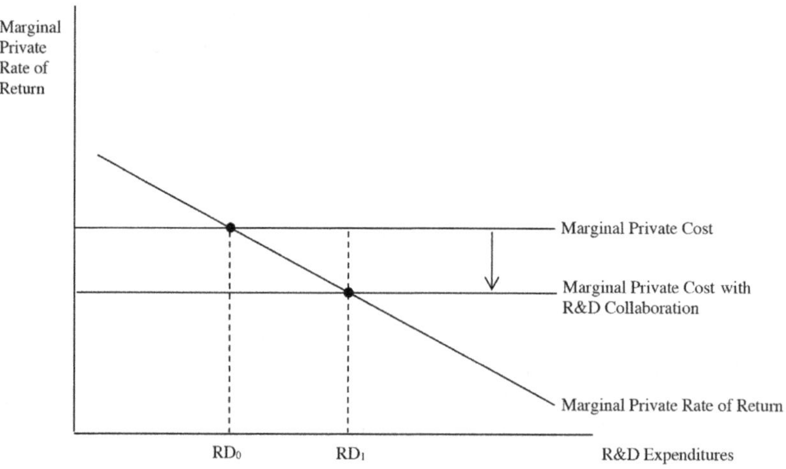

Figure 5.5 The economics of collaborative R&D

Intensity of R&D Collaboration

Most countries have environments conducive to collaboration in R&D. For example, Table 5.3 shows the percent of R&D active and non-R&D active firms engaged in collaboration in innovation.[11] The cross-country data in the table show that firms in the United Kingdom—R&D active firms as well as non-R&D active firms—engage in R&D collaboration to a greater extent than firms in the other countries shown in the table.

The data in Table 5.3 also show that the percent of collaborating firms is always greater for R&D active firms than for non-R&D active firms. This observation raises the question: Why do non-R&D active firms engage in R&D collaboration with other firms? Our answer is that they require technical research expertise for the adoption of others' technologies, but they do not have the internal capabilities to conduct the relevant foundational research. Through collaboration, they are able to acquire tacit knowledge relevant to their strategic needs.

The data in Table 5.3 also show that the United States is not listed among the OECD countries that provide data related to firms' engagement in collaborations in innovation, a point that we return to below.

Table 5.4 shows the percent of innovating firms collaborating in innovation with higher education or research institutions, by firm size. Innovation collaboration is not the same activity as R&D collaborations as our framework and previous discussion make clear. The data from Table 5.3 come from the OECD. The OECD definition of innovation collaboration, based on the source reference in the table, is:

> Innovation collaboration involves active participation with other organisations in joint innovation projects (i.e., those aimed at introducing a new or significantly improved product or process), but excludes pure contracting out of innovation-related work. It can involve the joint implementation of innovations with customers and suppliers, as well as partnerships with other firms or organisations.

Table 5.3 *Percent of R&D active and non-R&D active firms engaging in collaboration in innovation, by R&D status, years 2008–2010*

Country	R&D Active Firms (%)	Non-R&D Active Firms (%)
Australia	27.40	23.40
Austria	64.03	35.21
Belgium	50.84	28.44
Brazil	25.21	7.74
Chile	22.11	9.86
Czech Republic	44.21	15.80
Denmark	62.15	33.33
Estonia	51.27	26.73
Finland	46.18	11.69
France	58.23	25.64
Germany	32.14	15.80
Hungary	56.09	26.42
Ireland	36.78	14.90
Israel	50.94	30.15
Italy	19.56	4.62
Japan	56.95	26.97
Korea	33.02	32.84
Luxembourg	39.40	22.84
Netherlands	41.39	20.77
New Zealand	38.83	20.95
Norway	37.43	9.18
Poland	50.69	22.49
Portugal	30.70	8.32
Russian Federation	58.42	29.84
Slovak Republic	39.61	28.28
Slovenia	55.59	24.02
South Africa	38.98	17.03
Spain	39.19	11.66
Sweden	48.95	22.07
Switzerland	38.39	NA
Turkey	28.75	14.22
United Kingdom	77.87	50.06

Source: http://dx.doi.org/10.1787/888932891340 (accessed November 10, 2020).
Note: There are a few exceptions for the year of the data corresponding to 2008–2010. See the original source for these exceptions.

Table 5.4 *Percent of product and/or process innovating firms collaborating on innovation with higher education or research institutions, by size, years 2012–2014*

Country	SMEs (%)	Large Firms (%)
Australia	2.75	6.24
Austria	21.36	58.00
Belgium	21.68	49.68
Brazil	4.47	21.91
Chile	3.76	5.56
Czech Republic	11.64	31.07
Denmark	15.04	44.32
Estonia	19.71	23.64
Finland	21.31	68.77
France	12.87	37.42
Germany	13.65	39.83
Greece	9.43	42.94
Hungary	11.73	29.89
Iceland	12.96	19.44
Japan	12.89	23.62
Korea	6.75	5.84
Latvia	6.84	19.42
Netherlands	15.52	34.14
New Zealand	4.44	14.73
Norway	16.74	50.80
Poland	12.44	28.47
Portugal	9.18	38.33
Slovak Republic	11.06	33.68
Slovenia	21.27	44.44
Spain	15.86	35.52
Switzerland	9.73	22.86
Turkey	10.38	21.59
United Kingdom	23.99	26.97

Source: http://dx.doi.org/10.1787/888933619068 (accessed November 9, 2020).
Note: A small and medium sized enterprise (SME) is generally classified as having fewer than 250 employees. There are a few exceptions for the year of the data corresponding to 2008–10. See the original source for these exceptions.

Referring to the definition of innovation from Chapter 1, innovation collaboration involves bringing a new or improved product or process to market; it does not involve the creation of that product or process be it technology related or not. Nevertheless, our point in mentioning this form of collaboration here juxtaposed to our discussion of R&D collaboration is to emphasize again that the United States is not listed in the table. The United States does not collect data systematically on collaborative research activities or on innovative activities as defined by the OECD definition above or by a similar NSF definition.

This history of R&D collaboration in the United States has its contemporary origin in portions of President Jimmy Carter's Domestic Policy Review.[12] As we have mentioned, President Carter commissioned the Review in response to the productivity slowdown that the United States was beginning to experience in the early 1970s and then again in the late 1970s. When embargoed on October 31, 1979, from the Office of the White House Secretary to the Congress of the United States, one of President Carter's charges to Congress was:

> I am today announcing measures which will ensure our country's continued role as a world leader in industrial innovation. These initiatives address nine critical areas [one of which is] clarifying anti-trust policy … By spurring competition, anti-trust policies can provide a stimulant to the development of innovation. In some cases, however, such as in research, industrial cooperation may have clear social and economic benefits for the country. Unfortunately, our anti-trust laws are often mistakenly viewed as preventing all cooperative activity. The Department of Justice, at my direction, will issue a guide clearly explaining its position on collaboration among firms in research, as part of a broader program of improved communication with industry by the Justice Department and the Federal Trade Commission. This statement will provide the first uniform anti-trust guidance to industrial firms in the area of cooperation in research.

In November 1980, the U.S. Department of Justice (USDOJ) issued a report entitled *Antitrust Guide Concerning Research Joint Ventures*.[13] Therein it is stated that (USDOJ, 1980, p. 3):

> In general, the closer the joint activity is to the basic end of the research spectrum … the more likely it is to be acceptable under the antitrust laws.

This USDOJ opinion set the stage for the passage of the National Cooperative Research Act (NCRA) of 1984 which offered ways through which private-sector firms could engage in collaborative R&D and avoid aspects of antitrust violations.[14]

To date, there is not an official count of R&D collaborations among firms in the United States. Independently, researchers have estimated the number of joint research ventures over time, but as explained in Link (2020a, 2021a), those estimates are only estimates.

CONCLUDING OBSERVATIONS

In this chapter we identified two elements of what we call the "Technology policy environment." These elements are themselves not per se technology policies, although a case could be made that at one time they were. Today, patent systems and an environment, legal or otherwise, conducive to collaboration in R&D provide incentives for firms to increase their level of investments in R&D. As noted above, in Chapter 8 we will blend the two technology policy elements discussed in this chapter into what we call the "Technology policy ecosystem."

NOTES

1. In Chapter 8, we will blend the elements of the "Technology policy environment" with relevant actors to form the "Technology policy ecosystem."
2. See http://www.museumsinflorence.com/musei/cathedral_of_florence.html (accessed July 24, 2020).
3. Kwong (2014) substantiates this event.
4. See also Khan and Sokoloff (2004).
5. The original European Patent Convention is available at https://www.epo.org/law-practice/legal-texts/html/epc/2016/e/EPC_conv_20200701_en_20200620.pdf (accessed November 11, 2020).
6. Of course, obtaining a patent and protecting a patent are not costless activities, so the firm's marginal private cost schedule might also increase. We assume that this increase will not be offset by the economic gains from the increase in the marginal private rate of return schedule.
7. The economics of patenting literature perhaps needs a wider consideration of such issues as the impact on technological progress, competition, and the use of patents for non-market purposes (see Arvanitis, 1997; Doh et al., 2012; Hussinger, 2006; Turner, 1966).
8. The generalizations that follow are based on Link (2020a, 2021a).
9. Motohashi's (2005) study of Japanese university with industry collaborations also affirms that smaller firms benefit from more collaborations through higher levels of productivity than do larger firms.
10. See also Link (2021a).
11. The following data come from the OECD. The OECD definition of collaboration is: "Collaboration involves active participation in joint innovation projects with other organisations […] but excludes pure contracting out of innovation-related work. It can involve the joint implementation of innovations with customers and suppliers, as well as partnerships with other firms or organisations." See http://dx.doi.org/10.1787/888932891340 (accessed November 10, 2020).
12. A more detailed history is in Link (2020a).
13. Bozeman et al. (1986) and Link and Bauer (1989) developed a model that demonstrated that an output from research cooperation is additional R&D and that this

additional R&D is toward the basic research end of the R&D spectrum. Leyden and Link (2015) expanded this conclusion in terms of a game theoretic model by using a neoclassical equilibrium approach to illustrate the implications from free riding versus cooperation.

14. See Leyden and Link (2015) and Link (2020a) for the details of the National Cooperative Research Act of 1984 and its amendments.

6. Technology policies to leverage public-sector R&D

INTRODUCTION

Private-sector investments in R&D are focused primarily on development (the D in R&D) and some on applied research; very little private-sector R&D is focused on basic or fundamental research. We emphasize the character of use of R&D, meaning the basic research, applied research, and development categories, because private-sector investments in basic research are highly correlated with the productivity growth of private-sector firms and thus with economic growth. And much of the research that takes place in the public sector is basic research.

Basic research is generally conducted in universities and in Federal or national laboratories (we will rely on the term national laboratories throughout this book for consistency) although in many European countries, national laboratories are not as prevalent as they are in the United States. The appropriate counterpart term in many European countries is *Publicly Funded Research Organizations* (PROs), although within this group of organizations are universities as well as government research laboratories and institutions.

From a technology policy perspective, the focus of this chapter is how the technical knowledge generated through public-sector funded research in universities and in national laboratories enters, figuratively speaking, the development process for new technology in private-sector firms. Basically, technical knowledge through public-sector funded research complements private-sector investments in R&D. Were it not for such transfers of knowledge from the public sector, private-sector firms would have to increase, if they could, their investments in R&D to achieve the same level of technological knowledge that they receive as a result of knowledge transfer. Understanding these relationships is fundamental for understanding the extant technology policies that leverage the impact of public-sector R&D on private-sector R&D.

An emphasis in this book is on R&D in private-sector firms as the primary target variable for technology policy. Thus, our goal in this chapter is not only to make a case that technical knowledge generated through public-sector

R&D affects the private-sector R&D process, but also to describe technology policies that enhance public-sector R&D.

We will be using the term *knowledge transfer* throughout this chapter and not the term *technology transfer*. We use the term *knowledge transfer* to refer to the transfer of technical knowledge although we will not always use the adjective *technical* in our discussions even though the knowledge transferred from the public sector to the private sector that is relevant to our theme of technology policy is of a technical nature.

Recall from Chapter 1 (see Table 1.1) that we defined technology, as it relates to the private sector, as "the application of new knowledge, learned through science, to some practical problem." This application process occurs through private-sector R&D, and thus knowledge transfers from the public sector enhance the process of applying new knowledge to some practical problem.

To understand the process of knowledge transfer from universities and national laboratories to private-sector firms, one must understand the mechanisms used to transfer knowledge as well as the policy incentives that universities and national laboratories face to engage in knowledge transfer. As we explain this process, we also emphasize that not all knowledge transfer from the public sector to private-sector firms is a result of purposeful technology policy. Much of it occurs through the laws of the supply and demand of per se knowledge. The extent to which knowledge transfers occur from universities and national laboratories to private-sector firms depends on the incentives in place for private-sector firms to interact with university and national laboratories (i.e., the demand for knowledge to be transferred from the public sector) as well as the incentives in place for universities and national laboratories to interact with private-sector firms (i.e., the supply of knowledge to be transferred to the private sector).

There are both demand-side incentives and supply-side incentives for knowledge transfer interactions between private-sector firms and both universities and national laboratories. On the demand side, there is an economic cost to a private-sector firm for acquiring and using new knowledge, regardless of its source. These costs include the search cost of identifying sources of relevant knowledge and the cost of having to develop the internal capacity to absorb and use the relevant knowledge—the academic literature refers to investments in this internal capacity by the term *absorptive capacity*.

On the supply side, there are economic costs to universities and national laboratories to generate and distribute new knowledge. The generation of new knowledge is, in all likelihood, part of the professional responsibility of university faculty and national laboratory researchers. The distribution methods of such new knowledge are, to an extent, a matter of policy. For example, the EU uses its Framework Programme as the main mechanism to involve public-research organizations and industry partners to pursue basic and applied research (see Nepelski and van Roy, 2020; Nepelski et al., 2019).

To understand the genesis of relevant policy incentives for universities to distribute new knowledge, that is, to engage in knowledge transfers, one must look to the passage of the University and Small Business Patent Procedure Act of 1980 in the United States, which is commonly known as the Bayh-Dole Act of 1980. To understand the relevant policy incentives for national laboratories to engage in knowledge transfers, the story also begins in the United States with the passage of the Stevenson-Wydler Technology Innovation Act of 1980, which is commonly known as the Stevenson-Wydler Act of 1980.

The remainder of this chapter provides context for a discussion of these two U.S. legislative initiatives, which we refer to as technology policies to leverage public-sector R&D although we would be more accurate to refer to these technology policies as policies to incentivize the public sector to distribute knowledge, and how these technology policies have affected knowledge transfers from universities and national laboratories, respectively, to private-sector firms in the United States and in other countries with similar policies.

KNOWLEDGE TRANSFERS FROM UNIVERSITIES

R&D Activity in the Academic Sector

Universities and public research organizations are viewed by policy makers and national governments as important institutional actors in creating and exploiting knowledge (see Berbegal-Mirabent et al., 2013; Cunningham and Menter, 2020a, 2020b; Hewitt-Dundas, 2012; Wu, 2007). For the United Kingdom, enhancing university with firm research cooperation has been an ongoing policy challenge that has been the focus of no fewer than 15 policy reviews from 2003 to 2015, beginning with the Review of Business-University Collaboration conducted by Sir Richard Lambert in 2003 (see Dowling, 2015). The challenge facing the United Kingdom in relation to university with firm cooperation is outlined by Dowling (2015, p. 15) as follows:

> Ensuring the UK innovation system is able to support productive collaborations between universities and businesses is therefore key to enabling the world class research produced by our universities to be harnessed to support the business innovation which results in broader economic returns for both individual firms and the UK as a whole.

This challenge has led universities to put in place different internal organizational structures to support effective knowledge transfers such as technology transfer offices, internal research institutions, and cooperative research centers (see Dolan et al., 2019). This challenge has also led to universities pursuing different institutional strategies to support knowledge transfer activities (Giuri et al., 2019). The academic literature that is focused on entrepreneurial universities has addressed how universities respond to expanding their third mission to foster innovative activities while still pursuing their other missions of teaching and research (see Brown, 2016; Clark, 1998; Guerrero et al., 2014; Kirby, 2006).[1]

From a U.S. perspective, before discussing the purpose of the Bayh-Dole Act of 1980, that is, before discussing technology policy to leverage public-sector R&D, we set the stage by presenting and describing investments in R&D in the higher education or academic (hereafter academic) sector. Figure 6.1 shows the gross domestic R&D performed in the academic sector in the United Kingdom from 1981 through 2018, and Figure 6.2 shows gross domestic R&D in the academic sector in the United States from 1981 through 2018. In general, the trend over time in both countries has been positive, although the level of investment has flattened out somewhat, especially in the United Kingdom, in the post-Great Recession (2009 and 2010) period.

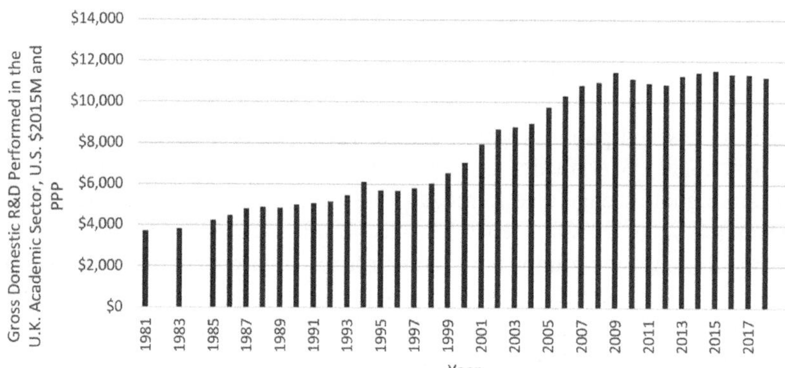

Source: https://www.oecd.org/sti/inno/researchanddevelopmentstatisticsrds.htm (accessed November 11, 2020).

Figure 6.1 *Gross domestic R&D performed in the U.K. academic sector, years 1981–2018, U.S. $2015M and PPP*

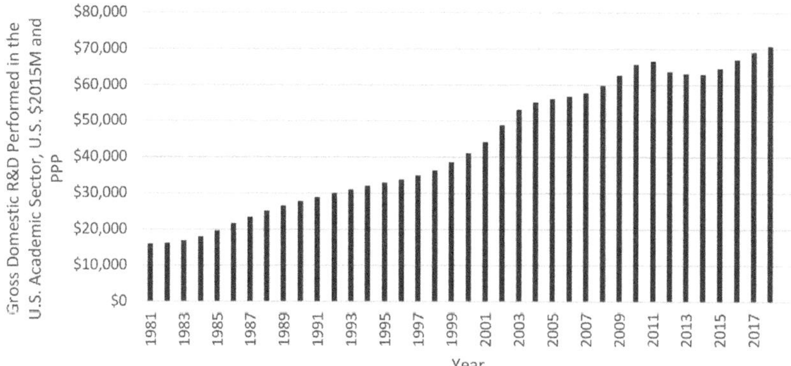

Source: https://www.oecd.org/sti/inno/researchanddevelopmentstatisticsrds.htm (accessed November 11, 2020).

Figure 6.2 Gross domestic R&D performed in the U.S. academic sector, years 1981–2018, U.S. $2015M and PPP

The amount of gross domestic R&D performed in the academic sector in various countries in year 2017 is shown in column (1) in Table 6.1. Following the United States, Germany and Japan are the two countries that invest the most in R&D in the academic sector. U.S. investments in R&D in the academic sector are more than three times those in Germany and Japan and more than six times those in the United Kingdom.[2]

In relative terms, the amount of gross domestic R&D performed in the private sector in the United Kingdom is nearly three times that performed in the academic sector in year 2017 (see Table 2.3 and Table 6.1). And the amount of gross domestic R&D performed in the private sector in the United States is more than five times that performed in the academic sector in year 2017 (see Table 2.3 and Table 6.1).

The percent of gross domestic R&D performed in the academic sector that is funded by the government, by country, is shown in column (2) in Table 6.1. At the top of the list is Mexico with 94 percent of R&D performed in the academic sector being funded by the government. In the United Kingdom, 62 percent of academic performed R&D is funded by the government, and in the United States that percent is slightly more than 56. Of course, much of the R&D conducted in the academic sector across most, if not all countries is basic research, and basic research has a public good characteristic. It is thus appropriate for the public sector, that is, the government, to support such activity for the commonweal.

In column (1) of Table 6.2 is the amount of gross domestic R&D performed in the academic sector. In column (2) is the amount of basic research performed in the academic sector, and in column (3) is the percent of total R&D performed in the academic sector that is basic research (column (2) divided by column (1)).

Table 6.1 *R&D performed in the academic sector, by country in year 2017, U.S. $2015M and PPP*

Country	(1) R&D Performed ($)	(2) Percent of R&D Performed in the Academic Sector Funded by the Government (%)
Australia	7,216.8	
Austria	3,085.1	85.41
Belgium	2,843.8	63.18
Canada	11,130.1	54.38
Chile	683.4	56.08
Czech Republic	1,335.2	84.40
Denmark	2,874.0	74.11
Estonia	212.9	68.96
Finland	1,711.0	80.04
France	12,818.8	79.60
Germany	21,730.2	82.48
Greece	944.0	65.91
Hungary	495.4	78.19
Iceland	119.5	81.32
Israel	1,509.6	67.19
Italy	7,457.8	79.95
Japan	20,325.7	52.10
Korea	7,476.3	77.65
Latvia	124.6	62.58
Lithuania	283.0	68.48
Luxembourg	162.6	93.05
Mexico	3,865.3	94.40
Netherlands	5,470.5	76.19
New Zealand	616.9	60.00
Norway	2,253.7	90.08
Poland	3,752.0	82.81
Portugal	1,821.1	80.53
Slovak Republic	373.4	81.33
Slovenia	147.6	70.80
Spain	5,635.3	71.63
Sweden	4,224.2	74.41
Switzerland	5,092.3	81.67
Turkey	7,185.6	57.20
United Kingdom	11,343.0	62.06
United States	69,217.1	56.25

Source: https://www.oecd.org/sti/inno/researchanddevelopmentstatisticsrds.htm (accessed November 11, 2020).

Table 6.2 *R&D performed in the academic sector allocated to basic research for year 2017, U.S. $2015M and PPP*

Country	(1) R&D Performed ($)	(2) Basic Research Performed ($)	(3) Percent of R&D Performed in the Academic Sector for Basic Research (%)
Austria	3,085.1	1,653.2	53.59
Belgium	2,843.8	512.8	18.03
Chile	683.4	346.5	50.70
Czech Republic	1,335.2	798.7	59.81
Denmark	2,874.0	1,203.5	41.88
Estonia	212.9	111.3	52.30
France	12,818.8	8,632.2	67.34
Greece	944.0	544.0	57.63
Hungary	495.4	296.8	59.90
Iceland	119.5	69.8	58.45
Israel	1,509.6	1,029.7	68.20
Italy	7,457.8	4,180.7	56.06
Japan	20,325.7	7,693.4	37.85
Korea	7,476.3	2,757.7	36.89
Latvia	124.6	60.2	48.29
Lithuania	283.0	130.4	46.05
Luxembourg	162.6	161.2	99.18
Mexico	3,865.3	1,468.7	38.00
Netherlands	5,470.5	3,098.2	56.64
New Zealand	616.9	348.3	56.46
Norway	2,253.7	927.9	41.17
Poland	3,752.0	2,807.4	74.82
Portugal	1,821.1	805.0	44.21
Slovak Republic	373.4	291.3	78.01
Slovenia	147.6	91.0	61.64
Spain	5,635.3	2,743.8	48.69
Switzerland	5,092.3	3,967.0	77.90
United Kingdom	11,343.0	*3,779.6*	33.32
United States	69,217.1	43,037.4	62.18

Source: https://www.oecd.org/sti/inno/researchanddevelopmentstatisticsrds.htm (accessed November 11, 2020).
Note: The U.K. amount of basic research is for 2016; the 2017 datum is not available.

Figure 6.3 shows, for year 2017, the percent of R&D performed in the academic sector for basic research and the percent of R&D performed in the academic sector funded by the government, by country. On the basis of this figure, controlling for no country effects, there appears to be a cross-country relationship between these two metrics. In fact, the correlation coefficient between these two metrics is 0.353. A positive correlation is not unexpected because the government should be funding public goods, and basic research is the foundation of new technical knowledge and knowledge has public good characteristics.

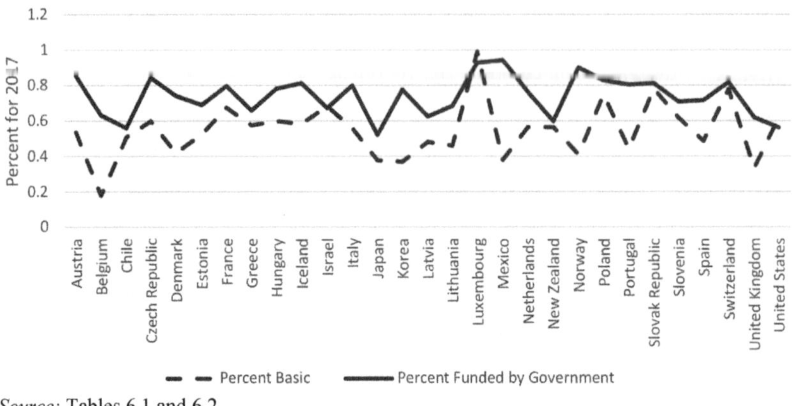

Source: Tables 6.1 and 6.2.

Figure 6.3 *Percent of R&D performed in the academic sector for basic research and the percent of R&D performed in the academic sector funded by the government, by country, for year 2017*

Scholarly publications are generally an expected output from academic R&D. Publishing is considered by many to be a professional responsibility of researchers, especially those employed in the academic sector. Table 6.3 shows the number of scientific and engineering (S&E) publications, by country, for the years 2006 and 2016 in columns (1) and (2), respectively. Also shown in Table 6.3 in column (3) is the average annual percentage change in the number of publications between the two years, as well as each country's year 2016 share of world publications. In year 2016, China ranked at the top of the list of the countries in terms of numbers of publications as shown in column (4), followed by the United States; the United Kingdom ranked fifth. China's top 2016 ranking accounted for over 18 percent of global S&E scholarly publications.

Table 6.3 *Publication of science and engineering articles by country, years 2006 and 2016*

Country (by 2016 total articles)	(1) 2006 Total Articles	(2) 2016 Total Articles	(3) Average Annual Change (%)	(4) 2016 World Total (%)
China	189,760	426,165	8.4	18.6
United States	383,115	408,985	0.7	17.8
India	38,590	110,320	11.1	4.8
Germany	84,434	103,122	2.0	4.5
United Kingdom	88,061	97,527	1.0	4.3
Japan	110,503	96,536	-1.3	4.2
France	62,448	69,431	1.1	3.0
Italy	50,159	69,125	3.3	3.0
South Korea	36,747	63,063	5.5	2.8
Russia	29,369	59,134	7.2	2.6
Canada	49,259	57,356	1.5	2.5
Brazil	28,160	53,607	6.6	2.3
Spain	39,271	52,821	3.0	2.3
Australia	33,100	51,068	4.4	2.2
Iran	10,073	40,974	15.1	1.8
Turkey	19,547	33,902	5.7	1.5
Poland	21,267	32,978	4.5	1.4
Netherlands	24,461	29,949	2.0	1.3
Taiwan	25,246	27,385	0.8	1.2
Switzerland	16,385	21,128	2.6	0.9
Malaysia	3,230	20,332	20.2	0.9
Sweden	16,634	19,937	1.8	0.9
Belgium	13,036	16,394	2.3	0.7
Czech Republic	8,839	15,963	6.1	0.7
Mexico	9,322	14,529	4.5	0.6
Portugal	7,136	13,773	6.8	0.6
Denmark	8,536	13,471	4.7	0.6
Austria	9,155	12,366	3.1	0.5
Israel	11,040	11,893	0.7	0.5
South Africa	5,636	11,881	7.7	0.5
Singapore	8,205	11,254	3.2	0.5
Egypt	3,958	10,807	10.6	0.5
Norway	7,093	10,726	4.2	0.5

Country (by 2016 total articles)	(1) 2006 Total Articles	(2) 2016 Total Articles	(3) Average Annual Change (%)	(4) 2016 World Total (%)
Greece	10,684	10,725	0.0	0.5
Finland	9,204	10,545	1.4	0.5
Romania	3,523	10,194	11.2	0.4
Thailand	4,270	9,581	8.4	0.4
Saudi Arabia	1,898	9,232	17.1	0.4
Pakistan	2,809	9,181	12.6	0.4
Argentina	5,600	8,648	4.4	0.4
Indonesia	619	7,729	28.7	0.3
New Zealand	5,607	7,465	2.9	0.3
Ukraine	5,296	7,375	3.4	0.3
Ireland	4,857	6,834	3.5	0.3
Chile	3,122	6,746	8.0	0.3
Hungary	5,530	6,208	1.2	0.3
Colombia	1,368	6,120	16.2	0.3
Slovakia	2,644	5,359	7.3	0.2
Tunisia	1,980	5,266	10.3	0.2
Algeria	1,288	4,447	13.5	0.2

Source: https://www.nsf.gov/statistics/2018/nsb20181/data/tables (accessed November 11, 2020).
Note: Academic researchers produce the bulk of all S&E articles; this table includes articles from all sectors.

The knowledge embodied in scholarly publications is, by definition, a part of the public domain. However, not all publications are relevant to a firm at a given point in time, and not all firms have the same level of ability to identify, much less absorb, the relevant knowledge from publications. Thus, there is an economic cost to firms acquiring knowledge through publications. There is an economic cost to universities to supply knowledge to the public domain through publications, and that cost is part of a university's research budget.

University with Firm Research Collaboration

University with firm research collaboration is not a new phenomenon, as discussed in Chapter 5. Both of the research collaborating partners enter into such agreements when it is beneficial to both parties. Different levels of satisfaction are experienced by both parties (see Suh et al., 2019) with trust and collaborative know-how playing a role in influencing university with firm research collaboration (see Bellini et al., 2019). Different organizational barriers on both sides can prevent research collaboration from being effective and thus prevent each party from realizing all potential benefits (see Valentin, 2000).

A study by Albats et al. (2018) highlights over the course of research collaboration how each party's evaluation of this activity changes. Based on a study of 33 countries, Davey and Galan-Muros (2020) found the vast majority of the study participants engage in collaborative R&D with less than 1 percent focusing on spin-off companies as part of their academic entrepreneurship activities. At the micro level some variations among firms in collaborations can occur due to the specific research focus of individual firm scientists and university faculty.[3]

Miller et al. (2018, p. 12) distinguished between academic entrepreneurship and entrepreneurial academics. An entrepreneurial academic is:

> An academic faculty member who adopts outlook, seeing opportunities to support their research objectives by engaging with commercial partners in a range of collaborative and less formal modes of engagement

And academic entrepreneurship is defined in terms of the behavior of faculty members. An academic entrepreneur is:

> An academic faculty member who undertakes technology commercialisation, using formal modes of engagement, that capitalise on specific market opportunities.

Such categorizations are important to understand at the micro level as researchers' engagement with firms will favor certain types of knowledge transfer activities and approaches to collaboration.

The EC sponsors the University-Business Cooperation in Europe Programme for the purpose of obtaining an understanding of R&D collaborations from the perspective of both universities (higher education institutions, HEIs) and firms. University with firm research collaboration is considered to be an engine toward the growth of knowledge-based economies, and that specific outcome was one of the motivations for the EC study. Through university with firm research collaboration, knowledge is transferred in both directions. Table 6.4 shows information from the EC's 2017 reports (one report from the university side and one report from the firm side) on university with firm research collaboration. The level of satisfaction with research collaboration of both universities and firms is shown in the table. The overall satisfaction index of firms in column (1) across countries is 28.2, and the overall satisfaction index of universities in column (2) across countries is 17. An overall country satisfaction index equals the difference between the percent of respondents who were willing to recommend collaboration with universities in R&D and the percent of respondents who were not willing to recommend collaboration with universities in R&D. Respondents could respond that they were passive, and if so that percent of respondents was not part of the satisfaction index.

Table 6.4 *Percent of firms and universities willing to recommend collaborations in R&D with universities and firms in R&D, year 2017*

Countries	(1) Overall Firm Satisfaction (%)	(2) Overall University Satisfaction (%)
Austria	31	17
Belgium	21	17
Bulgaria	0	32
Croatia	20	31
Czech Republic	33	19
Denmark	41	17
Estonia	11	34
Finland	43	34
France	13	0
Germany	34	3
Greece	31	49
Hungary	28	20
Ireland	33	23
Italy	35	25
Lithuania	24	13
Macedonia	16	56
Malta	33	33
Netherlands	22	29
Norway	17	-20
Poland	28	11
Portugal	30	35
Romania	26	42
Slovak Republic	-3	27
Slovenia	-10	35
Spain	37	40
Sweden	30	17
Turkey	57	55
United Kingdom	10	18

Source: http://www.ub-cooperation.eu/index/reports (accessed November 11, 2020).
Note: The overall country satisfaction index equals the difference between the percent of respondents who were willing to recommend collaboration with universities in R&D and the percent of respondents who were not willing to recommend collaboration with universities in R&D. Respondents could respond that they were passive.

Consider the case of the United Kingdom in year 2017. From the U.K. firm respondents, 36 percent were willing to recommend cooperation with universities and 26 percent were not; thus, the satisfaction index is +10 percent as shown in column (1). The rest of the firm respondents were passive about their experience with research cooperation. On the university side, the U.K. satisfaction index is +18 (similarly calculated) as shown in column (2).

Barriers to research collaboration satisfaction among U.K. firms and U.K. universities from the perspective of universities can be summarized from Table 6.5 by the following generalizations: a limited response to engage in collaborative research activity by firms and a lack of awareness of the nature of university research by firms. Barriers to research collaboration satisfaction among U.K. firms and U.K. universities from the perspective of firms can be summarized from Table 6.5 by the following generalizations: a lack of academics with business knowledge within the universities, a difference in the motivations for conducting research between firm scientists and university faculty, and a burdensome bureaucracy within universities for effective research cooperation. These findings concur with a U.K. centric literature review study by Vick and Robertson (2018) and from which they also found two distinct perspectives on motivations: sociopolitical and contextual. *The Dowling Review of Business-University Research Collaborations* (Dowling, 2015) identified the top ten barriers for firms and for universities.

Table 6.5 *United Kingdom barriers to collaboration: firm and university perspectives*

Ranked Firm Perspective	Ranked University Perspective
IP (intellectual property) and contract negotiations difficult to complete	University metric
Difficult to identify academic partners or academic capabilities	IP (intellectual property) and contract negotiations difficult to complete
Timescale difference	Academic time
Lack of funding	Lack of funding
Lack of objectives alignment	Not valued as part of academic career progression
Trust and mutual understanding	Lack of time/resource for networking or project development
Short-term focus rather than long-term R&D	Timescale difference
Other funding issues	Publishing and business concerns about competition
Low overall levels of business investment in R&D	Trust and mutual understanding
Lack of understanding within business of potential benefits of working with universities	Low overall levels of business investment in R&D

Source: https://www.raeng.org.uk/publications/reports/the-dowling-review-of-business-university-research (accessed November 8, 2020).

In post-conflict countries such as Bosnia and Herzegovina and Rwanda, the barriers to such research collaboration are more pronounced (see Brankovic, 2017; Nkusi et al., 2020). In small countries within Europe, Member States have taken different approaches to encourage and support research collaboration. In Ireland, for example, Knowledge Transfer Ireland was created to effectively support university, public research organization and firm collaboration for exploiting knowledge (see Cunningham et al., 2020). See Table 6.6.[4]

Table 6.6 Number of Irish underpinning intellectual property mechanisms from publicly funded research, years 2013–2019

IP Mechanism	2013	2014	2015	2016	2017	2018	2019
Patent	49	58	32	44	59	79	72
Software	53	53	74	63	55	71	35
Trade Secret	64	56	50	37	12	31	28
Copyright	5	17	8	17	8	4	13
Design Rights	2	5	4	0	0	3	35

Source: KTI Review and Annual Knowledge Transfer Survey (2019, p. 57), https://www.knowledgetransferireland.com/Reports-Publications/KTI-Annual-Review-Annual-Knowledge-Transfer-Survey-2019.pdf (accessed May 5, 2021).
Note: Shown in the table are the types of intellectual property (IP) that are the basis for licensing options and assignments from publicly funded research at universities and research performing organizations.

As discussed in Chapter 5, there are benefits associated with firm with firm collaboration in research. Extrapolating from the case of university with firm research collaboration in the United Kingdom and the quantitative satisfaction information presented in Table 6.4, we are hard pressed to generalize and thus recommend that European countries, or other countries for that matter, consider the adoption of any *direct* technology policies to leverage the effectiveness of public-sector R&D or private-sector R&D that involves the independent actions of universities and firms. However, there is preliminary information that the U.S. Bayh-Dole Act of 1980, and like legislation in other countries as discussed below, is an example of an *indirect* technology policy that might enhance technical knowledge transfers from universities to firms and thus leverage the effectiveness of public-sector R&D on private-sector R&D.

Collaboration through University Science and Research Parks

According to the EC (2008, p. 53), science and research parks (hereafter, science parks) fulfill an important role and at different levels:

- Science parks may provide the visibility and hence attraction to wider local strategies aiming at the creation of conditions for high-tech industries to prosper; cities and regions increasingly compete in seeking to become identified as the next "region of knowledge," "science region," or "creative region" to attract value-added jobs, and are hence looking for distinctive features.
- Science parks provide the advanced infrastructure on which research-intensive enterprises rely, besides the location factor, being often in close proximity to a university.
- Science parks can provide complementary services and support to local firms.
- Science parks are usually associated with strong, effective networking and higher levels of social capital.

We include a discussion of science parks in this chapter, even though most science parks are dominated by private-sector firm tenants conducting their own research, because many parks are tied administratively and/or geographically to universities. There are different categories of science parks: research, incubator, and cooperative parks (see Ng et al., 2019). A university science park is an infrastructure within the physical and administrative boundaries of a university in which firms can willingly locate an R&D facility that thereby enhances the transfer of tacit knowledge from university researchers, and possibly from researchers in other firms that are also located in the science park. Or, as defined by Link and Scott (2006, p. 44):[5,6]

> A university [science] park is a cluster of technology-based organizations that locate on or near a university campus in order to benefit from the university's knowledge base and ongoing research. The university not only transfers knowledge but expects to develop knowledge more effectively given the association with the tenants in the research park.

Phan et al. (2005, p. 166) offered the following definition:

> Science parks and business incubators are property-based organizations with identifiable administrative centers focused on the mission of business acceleration through knowledge agglomeration and resource sharing.

Table 6.7 List of university science parks, by country and region

Location	Number of Parks
Science Parks in Africa	
Ivory Coast	1
Madagascar	1
Senegal	2
Rwanda	1
South Africa	5
Zimbabwe	1
Science Parks in Western Europe	
Belgium	6
Denmark	5
Finland	24
France	60
Germany	13
Greece	4
Ireland	2
Italy	6
Luxembourg	1
Norway	2
Portugal	1
Spain	5
Sweden	12
Switzerland	7
Netherlands	6
Turkey	1
United Kingdom	63
Science Parks in Eastern Europe	
Austria	1
Czech Republic	2
Estonia	1
Latvia	1
Poland	4
Russia	3
Science Parks in the Middle East	
Algeria	5
Bahrain	2
Egypt	3
Israel	5

Location	Number of Parks
Iran	3
Jordan	3
Kuwait	1
Lebanon	1
Morocco	3
Oman	1
Qatar	1
Saudi Arabia	4
Syria	1
Tunisia	2
United Arab Emirates	1
Science Parks in Far Eastern Asia	
China	80
Hong Kong	2
Iran	16
Japan	23
Republic of Korea	3
Taiwan	3
Science Parks in Southeast Asia	
Malaysia	5
Singapore	1
The Philippines	3
Thailand	1
Vietnam	2
Science Parks in South Asia	
India	4
Science Parks in North America	
Canada	13
United States of America	72
Science Parks in South America	
Brazil	3
Ecuador	1
Panama	1
Republic Dominican	1
Science Parks in Australia and New Zealand	
Australia	9
New Zealand	1

Source: http://www.unesco.org/new/en/natural-sciences/science-technology/university-industry-partnerships/science-parks-around-the-world/ (accessed November 9, 2020).

The theoretical literature on the benefits to universities and firms from their relationship in a university science park is, however, greater than the empirical literature that quantifies such benefits.[7] As reviewed by Link and Scott (2018) and Link (2020b), the literature is thin on country-specific benefits.

To the best of our knowledge there is no complete accounting of the number of active university science parks on a country by country basis or even on a continent by continent basis. The United Nations Educational, Scientific and Cultural Organization (UNESCO) offers one accounting of the number of science parks as shown in Table 6.7. The absolute number of science parks shown in Table 6.7 might be interpreted as a testament to presumed benefits to both universities and firms from being co-located.[8]

It has been suggested that science parks are declining in their importance as a public-sector infrastructure to enhance R&D as well as regional growth (see Hobbs et al., 2020; Link, 2020b). Perhaps this decline was enhanced by the growth of other innovation cluster venues.

The term *clusters* or *innovation clusters* has been used by scholars from a number of disciplines to refer to various forms of technology and innovation infrastructures. These infrastructure forms include, using the contemporary vernacular, creative hubs, innovation districts, industrial districts, research precincts, growth centers, science and technology parks, and more (see Esmaeilpoorarabi et al., 2018).[9]

One often traces the broad concept of clusters to the scholarship of Alfred Marshall's discussion of industrial districts (see Marshall, 1919).[10] As noted by Belussi and Caldari (2009, pp. 336–7):

> "Industrial district" means an area where a concentration of firms has settled down; but, it is not simply a localised industry, as Marshall clarifies well, especially in his *Principles of Economics* … Through the passing of time and the development of the aspects enumerated above, the district acquires what Marshall calls a special atmosphere: it is this special atmosphere that gives the various advantages to the firms gathered together in a particular area.

Katz and Wagner (2014, pp. 1–2) define innovation districts as follows:

> [Innovation districts,] by our definition, are geographic areas where leading-edge anchor institutions and companies cluster and connect with start-ups, business incubators, and accelerators. They are also physically compact, transit-accessible, and technically-wired and offer mixed use housing, office, and retail … Innovation districts represent a radical departure from traditional economic development. Unlike customary urban revitalization efforts that have emphasized the commercial aspects of development (e.g., housing, retail, sports stadiums), innovation districts help their city and metropolis move up the value chain of global competitiveness by growing the firms, networks, and traded sectors that drive broad-based prosperity. Instead of building isolated science parks, innovation districts focus extensively

> on creating a dynamic physical realm that strengthens proximity and knowledge spillovers. Rather than focus on discrete industries, innovation districts represent an intentional effort to create new products, technologies and market solutions through the convergence of disparate sectors and specializations (e.g., information technology and bioscience, energy, or education).

Mulgan (2019) wrote about contemporary innovation districts:

> Today, innovation districts and clusters can be found across the globe in cities as diverse as Paris, Buenos Aires, and Montréal—with ambitious projects continuing to be launched in places like Singapore. Increasingly, smaller cities without institutions in the league of MIT [Massachusetts Institute of Technology] or Cambridge [Massachusetts], are also managing to foster successful districts; Chattanooga, Tennessee and Fort Worth, Texas are just two less known US examples … Some surprising places have done particularly well in fostering innovation districts: the district built around an anchor institution—Ruta N—in Medellin in Colombia is a stand-out example of their place in broader strategies of urban reinvention.

Perhaps innovation clusters are simply the next generation of co-located innovation hubs, and perhaps their importance or popularity will wane over time much like that of science parks.

The Bayh-Dole Act of 1980

The Bayh-Dole Act of 1980 was the first of several U.S. policy responses to the U.S. productivity slowdown discussed in Chapter 1. The purpose of the Bayh-Dole Act was to, among other things, ensure the utilization of inventions by private-sector firms arising from publicly supported R&D in universities.[11] This goal was to be accomplished through the transfer of intellectual property rights from the public sector, which funded the university research, to the universities, where the research was conducted. Thus, the universities would patent the technical knowledge or technology that resulted from the public-sector funded research, and that knowledge would be transferred to private-sector firms through patent licenses. This patent-based transfer of technical knowledge was facilitated through a university technology transfer office (TTO) or, as these offices are more commonly called today, a university office of commercialization.

The relevant and similar enabling legislation in the United Kingdom traces to the 1985 Kingman Letter. The Kingman Letter was sent from Sir John Kingman, Chairman of the Science and Engineering Research Council, to the vice chancellors and principals of the U.K. universities on May 14, 1985. The letter was offering the universities the opportunity to assume rights and responsibilities with regard to the exploitation of Research Council funded discoveries that were previously enjoyed by the British Technology Group (see Harvey, 1992). Motivating the Kingman Letter was the government's desire to encourage industrial and commercial applications of U.K. scientific and technological discoveries for the benefit of the economy.

Table 6.8 shows the countries that have adopted Bayh-Dole-like legislation since 1980 by year of adoption, and Figure 6.4 shows over time the cumulative proportion of countries that adopted Bayh-Dole-like legislation since 1980.[12]

Table 6.8 Countries that adopted Bayh-Dole-like policies, by year of adoption

Country (Year)	Policy Title
United States (1980)	Bayh-Dole Act
Spain (1983)	University Reform Law
United Kingdom (1985)	Kingman Letter
China (1994)	Measures for Intellectual Property Rights Made Under the Governmental Funding of the National High Technology Program
Denmark (1999)	The Act on Inventions at Public Institutions
France (1999)	Innovation Act
Japan (1999)	Industrial Revitalization Special Law (known as the Japanese Bayh-Dole Act)
South Korea (2000)	Technology Transfer Promotion Law
Italy (2001)	National Law 383/2001
Austria (2002)	Universitätsgesetz 2002 (UG 2002)
Germany (2002)	Employee Invention Law
Indonesia (2002)	Law No. 18 of 2002 on the National System of Research, Development and Application of Science and Technology
Mexico (2002)	Science and Technology Law
Norway (2003)	Proposition No. 67 of the Odelsting
Russia (2003)	Patent Law of 2003
Brazil (2004)	Innovation Law
Finland (2007)	Inventions Act
India (2008)	The Protection and Utilisation of Public Funded Intellectual Property Bill, 2008 (Indian Bayh-Dole Bill)
South Africa (2008)	Intellectual Property Rights from Publicly Financed Research and Development Act
Malaysia (2009)	Intellectual Property Commercialisation Policy for Research & Development Projects Funded by the Government of Malaysia
Philippines (2009)	Philippine Technology Transfer Act of 2009

Source: Gores and Link (2021).

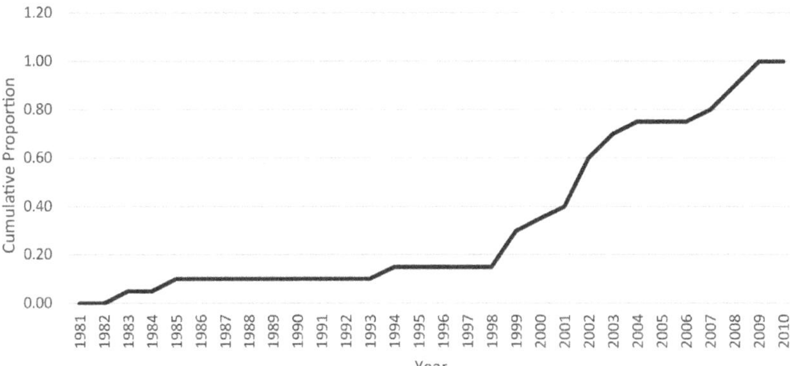

Source: Calculations based on data in Table 6.1.

Figure 6.4 *Cumulative proportion of countries with university-based technology transfer policies, years 1981–2010*

In the absence of the Bayh-Dole Act and its adoptions in other countries, technical knowledge would be transferred from universities to the private sector through publications, licenses to patented technologies, and the start-up of new companies. Data on such transfers of technical knowledge are codified in the United Kingdom through the public sector's Higher Education Business Interaction Survey administered by the government's UK Research and Innovation (UKRI). In the United States, similar data are collected through the private sector's AUTM Licensing Survey administered by the Association of University Technology Managers (AUTM).

With the Bayh-Dole Act and its adoptions in other countries, we contend that there is simply more of the same activity than would have existed in the absence of the Bayh-Dole Act. Thus, the Bayh-Dole Act, and its adoptions in other countries, is an example of technology policy that leverages the effectiveness of public-sector R&D on private-sector R&D. To the extent that the Bayh-Dole Act of 1980 in the United States, and to the extent that the Bayh-Dole Act like legislation in other countries, incentivized university faculty to shift their basic or fundamental research toward more applied research as a prerequisite for patenting, the end result on knowledge transfer will likely be two-pronged. One the one hand, the Bayh-Dole Act or similar legislation in other countries does not alter the scholarly publication-based reward system in universities. In fact, such legislation might indirectly have increased the rate of scholarly publication because academic references are a key part to document the usefulness of the patent applications. On the other hand, the Bayh-Dole Act or similar legislation will lead to an increase in university patenting due to the transfer of ownership from the government to the university, and patents are a prerequisite for patent licenses. Patent licenses embody knowledge, and while frequently referred to as a technology transfer mechanism, they are in fact a mechanism that embodies and thus transfers technical knowledge from the university to the licensee.[13]

Figure 6.5 shows the number of U.S. university patent applications and patent awards over time. Visually, the trend in both U.S. patent metrics is positive over time, although we have not taken into account the lag between a patent application and a patent award, if there was an award. There is in Figure 6.5 a slight decrease in the number of patent applications during the Great Recession of 2008 to 2009, but that decrease is less evident in the patent awards trend.

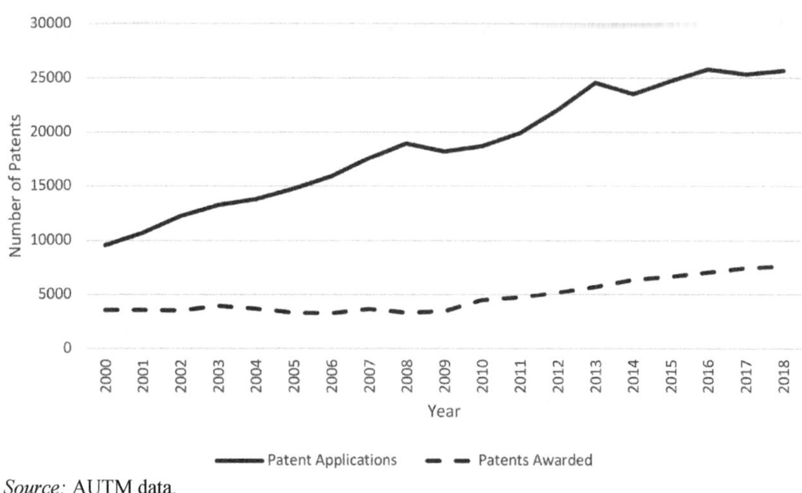

Source: AUTM data.

Figure 6.5 *U.S. university patent applications and patent awards, years 2000–2018*

KNOWLEDGE TRANSFERS FROM NATIONAL LABORATORIES

The knowledge transfer mechanisms from national laboratories are similar to those from universities. Specifically, research scientists in national laboratories publish their research and knowledge is also transferred through patent licenses. Data on knowledge transfers from the national laboratories in the United States are publicly available at the agency level, that is, the data from all of the laboratories operated by a U.S. agency are aggregated to the agency level. Each agency is legislated to provide such information to the Technology

Partnerships Office (TPO), which is administratively located at the National Institute of Standards and Technology (NIST). The TPO prepares an annual report for the President and the Congress based on information provided to it by the agencies.[14]

The United Kingdom and other countries (e.g., Belgium, Denmark, France, Ireland, Italy, Spain, and Switzerland) conduct an annual knowledge transfer survey from their PROs (which include universities). However, to the best of our knowledge, the United States is the only country that makes public knowledge transfer metrics exclusively from its national laboratories.[15]

In the United States, there was legislation similar to the Bayh-Dole Act of 1980 that encouraged knowledge transfers from national laboratories. The Stevenson-Wydler Act of 1980 transferred ownership of patented technology from the government to the national laboratory, and thus provided an incentive for laboratory scientists to patent more than prior to that legislation (and likely to publish more). Much like with the Bayh-Dole Act and universities, the Stevenson-Wydler Act is a technology policy in the sense that it leverages public-sector R&D in national laboratories and thus, through licensing, enhances private-sector R&D.

CONCLUDING OBSERVATIONS

In this chapter we identified two areas through which technology policy has an effect on private-sector R&D via public-sector R&D. One area is the knowledge transfers from universities that have been enhanced through the Bayh-Dole Act in the United States and Bayh-Dole-like legislation in a number of other countries, and the other area is the knowledge transfers from national laboratories that have been enhanced through the Stevenson-Wydler Act in the United States and perhaps enhanced through EC initiatives in other countries.

In Figure 6.6 we offer a more detailed framework for explaining the role of investments in R&D and the role of private-sector and public-sector technology policies. See the shaded cell in the figure. In Chapter 7, we expand the framework further by introducing cross-country innovation policies. Recall from Chapter 1 and Table 1.1 the definition of an innovation: "a technology put into use or commercialized." Thus, to anticipate this further expanded framework, the innovation policies that we discuss will focus on the transition from the cell in Figure 6.6 labeled "Greater level of new technology" to the cell labeled "Innovation."

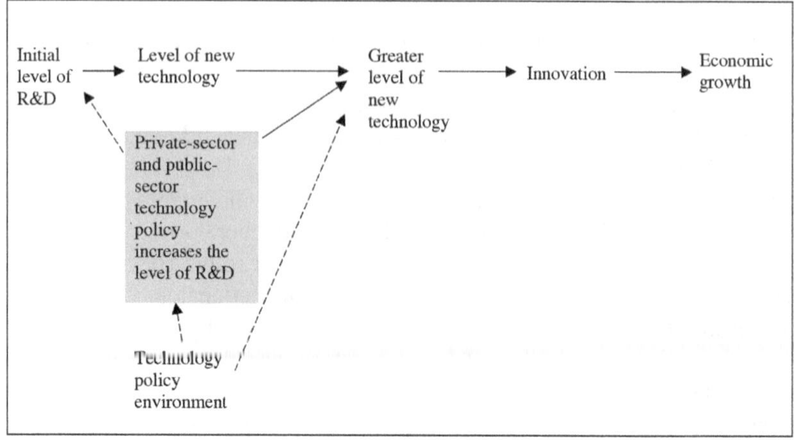

Source: Prepared by the authors.

Figure 6.6 Framework for explaining the role of investments in R&D and the role of technology policy and innovation policy in the economy

NOTES

1. Regarding the United Kingdom, universities earned over £1.1 billion from research collaboration with business of which £507 million comes from contract research and £163 million from intellectual property (IP) income for the years 2015/16 (HESA, 2017).
2. In Germany, for example, the major policy instrument is termed *The Excellence Initiative*. It played a significant role in shifting the academic sector's structure to focus on research and knowledge transfers (Civera et al., 2020; Cunningham and Menter, 2020a, 2020b; Lehmann and Stockinger, 2019; Menter et al., 2018).
3. For a U.S. perspective, see Hertzfeld et al. (2006).
4. Innovation vouchers were a policy instrument that both small countries, such as the Netherlands, Belgium, and Ireland, and large EU Member States used to support industry, particularly SME and university and public research organization (Cornet et al., 2006; Roper, 2008; Sala et al., 2016).
5. See also Link and Scott (2007).
6. The EC (2017b, p. 54) noted: "There are a number of types of science parks in Europe and over the world. There is also not only one definition for the science park. One of the reasons is that in different countries different forms of science parks have been developed. Each country has a different history of science parks and has its own terms. For instance, 'Science Park' is used in the United Kingdom, 'Technopole' or 'Technopolis' is used in France, 'Technology Centre' and/or 'Technology Park' is used in Germany, 'Research Park' as a term is mainly used in the U.S.A. etc."

7. The topics addressed by authors writing about science parks include the following: factors affecting firm decisions to locate on a park, the formation of university parks and university performance, firm performance on a park, and park and regional economic growth and development. See Hobbs et al. (2017).
8. Hobbs et al. (2020, pp. 42, 51) conclude their study of U.S. science parks in the following way: "We find that only 11 of 146 research and science parks in the USA have, in the spirit of public accountability, conducted an economic impact study [and] the 11 extant studies do show positive local, regional, and/or state impacts."
9. Esmaeilpoorarabi et al. (2018) provide an excellent taxonomy of various types of clusters.
10. Belussi and Caldari (2009, p. 336) used the phrase "father of the modern concept of Industrial District" with reference to Marshall.
11. A detailed discussion of the Bayh-Dole Act is also in Leyden and Link (2015).
12. A more detailed discussion of the Bayh-Dole-like legislation that was adopted in other countries is in Gores and Link (2021).
13. While there is not a lot of empirical support for our contention of the Bayh-Dole Act of 1980 and its adoption in other countries, there is empirical evidence that, at least in the United States, the number of university patents did increase in the post-1980 period and so did the number of university technology transfer offices. See Link and Van Hasselt (2019) and the references therein.
14. Much has been written about technology transfer activity from U.S. national laboratories. For example, see Link and Oliver (2020) and the references therein, and see Link (2021b). Regarding the organizational structure of national laboratories, see Gingrich et al. (2020).
15. See EC (2020).

7. Global innovation systems

This chapter summarizes many of the OECD's country reports on innovation policy and innovation systems:[1]

> OECD *Reviews of Innovation Policy* offer a comprehensive assessment of the innovation system of individual OECD member and partner countries, focusing on the role of government. They provide concrete recommendations on how to improve policies which impact on innovation performance, including R&D policies. Each review identifies good practices from which other countries can learn.

Our summary is presented in Table 7.1. From that table, we offer the following stylized observations that are noted in Table 7.2.[2]

Table 7.1 Major strengths of global innovation systems, by selected OECD country

Country	Major System Strengths
Austria (p. 46)	• Strong long-term economic performance, with high living standards and quality of life • A strong export-oriented manufacturing sector, upgrading within industries, with world-market leaders and innovators in various niches • Rapid advances in the provision of human resources, creation of the Universities of Applied Science • Rapid increase of research and development (R&D) intensity across most industries and firm size classes, achieving a leading position in the European Union (EU) • A large number of R&D-active firms, including many SMEs, that have significantly expanded their R&D capacity
Chile (p. 26)	• Stable macroeconomic framework and well-functioning product markets • International openness • Reliable regulatory and legal frameworks • Political commitment to increased support to innovation • Trustful relationship between government, public servants and the private sector

Country	Major System Strengths
Columbia (p. 49)	• Strong economic performance over most of the last decade • Strong political commitment to education and increasing participation rates • Strong commitment to strengthen innovation as a sustainable and inclusive driver of development • Some research institutions with strong research capacities and international linkages • Confidence, enthusiasm and willingness to innovate among the national STI [science, technology and innovation] policy leadership. Similar qualities at departmental and municipal levels in some areas
Costa Rica (p. 23)	• Geographical location favourable to value-chain integration with North America • Sound and stable macroeconomic environment • Strong base of multinational enterprises in advanced manufacturing industries and offshore and information services industries • Diversified export base • Multiple international trade agreements
Croatia (p. 48)	• Geographic location on the Adriatic coast and at the crossroads of central and southeastern Europe; historical links with several developed and emerging economies • Good macroeconomic performance prior to the crisis • Improvements in framework conditions for innovation (while significant scope remains), including in the institutional landscape of policy actors in STI [science, technology and innovation] matters • A well-educated population, especially in terms of secondary education attainment, and strengths in social sciences, law and humanities • Some strengths or pockets of excellence in public research (universities and PRIs) and examples of collaboration between academia and industry
Finland (p. 22)	• Political stability with clear rule of law, high levels of trust and a culture of Nordic-style "flexicurity" • Strong base in resource-based and certain manufacturing industries as well as ICT and related services • Strong, skilled, innovative and experienced ICT and new media communities able to diversify into new businesses and provide digitalisation expertise to existing businesses • High-skilled professionals (ICT, health tech, mechanical engineering) • An education system that is excellent at the school level and good at higher level

Country	Major System Strengths
France (p. 34)	• France offers top-quality, multi-skilled and innovative engineers for industry • A significant number of researchers are internationally recognised for their excellence, although the overall quality of French fundamental research is average • Some top-quality PROs operate in fields such as health and ICTs • France has a growing population of imaginative and skilled entrepreneurs • The country has easy conditions for business creation and effective policies encouraging the creation of young innovative firms
Hungary (p. 29)	• Robust medium-term growth of total factor productivity and GDP per capita resulting in convergence with more advanced countries • Strong growth of the manufacturing base • High degree of international openness • Generally well-skilled labour force • Good framework condition for innovation in many respects
Kazakhstan (p. 18)	• Rich natural resource endowments • Unique geographic position • Growing young population with international experience • Cultural diversity • Genuine commitment to improve and expand the science, technology and innovation system
Korea (p. 17)	• Strong, mobilising national vision • Relatively high growth of GDP, sound macro-economic policies • Strong government support for innovation • Relatively good framework conditions for innovation • High share of business spending on R&D in overall R&D
Lithuania (p. 17)	• Strong macroeconomic performance, leading to convergence • Largely favourable framework conditions for innovation and entrepreneurship • Favourable conditions for the establishment and development of start-ups • High share of tertiary graduates, including in science and technology (S&T) • Increased openness, transparency and stakeholder involvement in STI [science, technology and innovation] policy formulation
Luxembourg (p. 20)	• A high level of socio-economic development • An open economy, taking full advantage of its favourable location at the heart of Europe • A largely favourable regulatory environment and a responsive government • A dynamic and evolving research landscape • Improved research system governance as a result of consolidation and well-designed performance contracts
Malaysia (p. 22)	• Successful socio-economic development trajectory • Good business environment and well-developed infrastructure • Rich natural resource endowment and biodiversity • A coherent vision for the country; well-designed and comprehensive strategic plans • Capacity to launch comprehensive and ambitious (cross-) sectoral reforms

Country	Major System Strengths
Netherlands (p. 25)	• Successful long-term socio-economic performance • Strong export performance • Strong human resource base • Overall good framework conditions for innovation including solid institutions and a supportive business environment • Tight integration in the global economy. Multinationals with global research, including in R&D and innovation
New Zealand (p. 11)	• The basic conditions for entrepreneurship and innovation are good • Most aspects of framework conditions are conducive to innovation • Government is aware of the importance of science and technology in escaping the "low productivity trap" and social acceptance of science and technology in and outside the workplace is satisfactory by international standards • A predictable policy environment and a competent public administration which aims to take a rigorous approach to the rationale for government intervention [i.e., market failure]
Norway (p. 10)	• Competitive natural-resource-based sectors, most importantly oil and gas • A dynamic high-performing private services sector • Disciplined and forward-looking economic policy • Sound microeconomic management and competition policy • A highly educated labour force
Peru (p. 35)	• Sound and stable macroeconomic environment • Strong export-oriented resource-based industries • Existence of some well designed and managed funds support programmes that highlight the existence of latent R&D, S&T [science and technology] and innovation potential and catalyse the development of research, development and innovation (RDI) activities • Performing technology transfer institutions • Pockets of excellence in scientific research
Russian Federation (p. 16)	• Generous endowment of natural resources and accumulated intellectual capital • Geographical proximity to, and historical links with, many advanced and emerging countries • High general level of education of the population. A well developed and recently reinforced higher education system in science and technology which attracts a large but decreasing share of enrolments • Long-standing scientific and engineering culture and many centres of world excellence in the modernised part of the public research system. International reputation and even prestige in key S&T fields, such as aerospace, nuclear science and engineering, and advanced software • An increasing number of firms, including a significant proportion of fast-growing ones, with best practice production and management methods capable of seizing new market opportunities through innovation when incentives are sufficient. A critical mass of new technology-based firms in some sectors and locations

Country	Major System Strengths
Slovenia (p. 32)	• Successful socio-economic development and good record in economic performance • Leading new EU member state on many economic and innovation-related indicators • Strong endowment in scientific talent and culture of research • Clusters of excellence in academic and industrial research • Substantial increases in the numbers and quality of scientific publications
South Africa (p. 11)	• Resource-based industries and related knowledge-intensive business services (KIBS) • Knowledge infrastructure, albeit small in relation to the size of the overall population • High proportion of business enterprise expenditure on R&D (BERD) and gross expenditures on R&D (GERD) • Traditional linkages between major industries and the knowledge infrastructure • International industrial and academic networks
Sweden (p. 49)	• Successful economic development • Specialised at high end of global value chains • Good framework conditions for innovation • A strong human resource base • High investment in R&D, KBC and information and communication technology (ICT)
Switzerland (p. 51)	• Strong industry (large and small firms), good framework conditions • Many sectors of Swiss industry (and services) strong in innovation, high level of industrial research • Very good university sector • Strong research infrastructure • Strong academic output (people, publications, etc.) and impact
Vietnam (p. 25)	• Strong economic growth performance, increases in income and diminishing poverty levels. Vietnam's dynamism over more than two decades appears very favourable in international comparisons • A privileged geographical location in one of the world's most dynamic regions, with access and proximity to large and increasingly integrated regional markets and increasing knowledge flows • A sizeable labour force and favourable demographics. Although the working population has begun to age, Vietnam will continue to benefit from a demographic bonus for some time • A substantial national effort on education. This is bearing fruit, as the country performs better than countries with similar income in terms of primary/secondary enrolments, secondary student performance and adult literacy rates • Attractiveness for investment by multinational enterprises, which transfer more advanced and modern production and management methods

Source: Prepared by the authors based on https://www.oecd.org/innovation/oecd-reviews-of-innovation-policy.htm (accessed November 12, 2020).
Note: The page number in the corresponding OECD report is given in parentheses. The OECD reports list more than five strengths; the first five listed are considered herein to be the major strengths.

Table 7.2 *Characteristics of the major strengths of global innovation systems, by selected OECD country*

Country	R&D Activity is a Strength	Academic/ Research Sector is a Strength	New Technology is the Basis for Innovation	Educated/ Scientific Labor Force is a Strength	Importance of the Role of the Public Sector
Austria	√	√		√	
Chile					√
Columbia		√			√
Costa Rica					
Croatia	√	√		√	√
Finland		√	√	√	√
France		√		√	√
Hungary				√	
Kazakhstan					√
Korea	√				√
Lithuania				√	√
Luxembourg		√			√
Malaysia					√
Netherlands	√			√	√
New Zealand				√	√
Norway	√			√	√
Peru	√	√			√
Russian Federation		√		√	
Slovenia		√		√	
South Africa	√	√			
Sweden	√			√	
Switzerland		√		√	
Vietnam			√	√	

Source: Table 7.1.

While some countries in Table 7.2 have more √ marks than others, one should not interpret that fact to mean that those countries are more innovative than the others. Counts of √ marks do not necessarily reflect the quality of a country's innovation policies.

Our subjective interpretation of the objective information in Table 7.2 is that our framework in Figure 7.1 for explaining the role of investments in R&D and the role of private-sector and public-sector technology policies has aspects of construct validity. Our initial view was that a country with an advancing or even advanced innovation policy would not explicitly point out its adherence to the paradigm:

$$R\&D \rightarrow technology \rightarrow innovation \rightarrow economic\ growth$$

Rather, our perception after completing Figure 7.1 is that our framework is relevant and might serve as a benchmark for other developing countries.

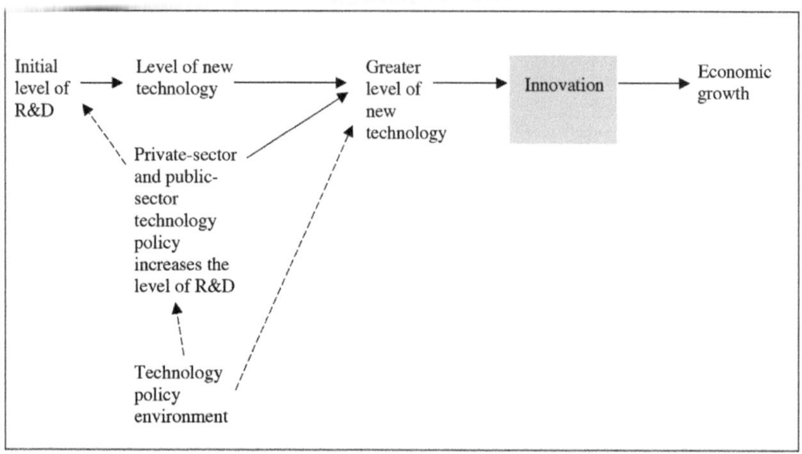

Source: Prepared by the authors.

Figure 7.1 *Expanded framework for explaining the role of investments in R&D and the role of private-sector and public-sector technology policies*

CONCLUDING OBSERVATIONS

The European Union publishes an annual comparative *Innovation Scorecard* for each Member State along with other non-Member States such as Norway, Ukraine, Switzerland.[3] This *Innovation Scorecard* identifies the key strengths and weaknesses and provides comparative insights for stakeholders within and outside EU Member States. Acknowledging the limitations with respect to our analysis, it does however further affirm that countries possess different varieties of strengths with respect to innovation characteristics. Table 7.2 provides an illumination of such varieties. The core policy making challenge for both policy makers and legislators is knowing the major strengths a country possesses and, given this knowledge, how best to focus policy interventions and instruments to realize desired policy outcomes that will effectively influence macro and micro level actor decisions and behaviors. Attendant questions are thus: Is the policy focus on further enhancing existing strengths? Is the focus on developing weaker innovation characteristics in order to reach international threshold norms? What distinctive and enduring characteristics should be developed to anticipate future needs and demands? These are challenging and searching questions for policy makers and are set against, as well as guided by, national ambitions with respect to technology and innovation in an international context. Many national technology policy and innovation policy statements and strategies convey ambitions with respect to being world class and/or internationally excellent or being the best in the world. This chapter also highlights that to realize such policy ambitions requires major strengths across a range of innovation characteristics. Creating and maintaining such strengths can take years to solidify. In realizing such policy ambitions, there is a temporal aspect because other countries can nullify major strengths or even emulate proven policy interventions in an accelerated manner.

NOTES

1. See https://www.oecd.org/innovation/oecd-reviews-of-innovation-policy.htm (accessed November 12, 2020).
2. The √ marks in Table 7.2 reflect our effort for an objective reading of the related OECD reports. The absence of a √ mark does not necessarily mean that the noted characteristic of a country's innovation system or innovation policies is not important. That characteristic was simply not among the top five listed in the OECD report.
3. See https://ec.europa.eu/growth/industry/policy/innovation/scoreboards_en.

8. Toward a technology/innovation policy ecosystem

INTRODUCTION

In the preceding chapters, we developed a framework for explaining the role of investments in R&D and the role of private-sector and public-sector technology policies. That framework is presented here as Figure 8.1.

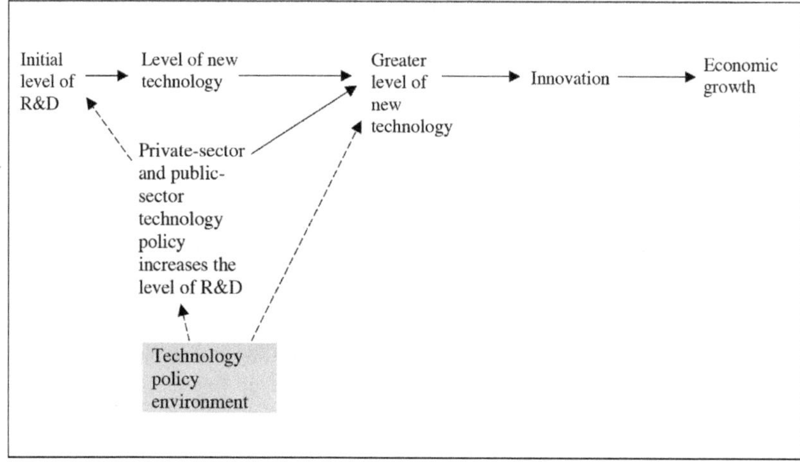

Source: Prepared by the authors.

Figure 8.1 Framework for explaining the role of investments in R&D and the role of private-sector and public-sector technology policies with an emphasis on the technology policy environment

As we have discussed the different facets of technology policy in various countries, it has become clear that there are significant differences with respect to the private sector's and the public sector's commitment to the objectives of a country's policy agency. We view this last statement as a statement of fact rather than a statement of criticism because it is based in large part on our objective accounting (i.e., through data) of the strengths of innovation systems across OECD countries as summarized in Table 7.2.

In this concluding chapter we reflect on the framework in Figure 8.1, and our reflection is based on the complexity of and differences in the technology policies in various countries that influence the innovation policies in those countries as reflected in part through the country by country differences revealed in Table 7.2. Our reflection has brought about the question: Why do countries differ in the effectiveness of their innovation policies as reflected through the effectiveness of their technology policies (i.e., as reflected through their private-sector and public-sector levels of investment in R&D)?

The answer to this question is that the previous chapters treated technology policy independent of an innovation ecosystem in which a policy is formulated and implemented. That is, the previous chapters *only* (our emphasis) focused on institutional infrastructure differences among countries.

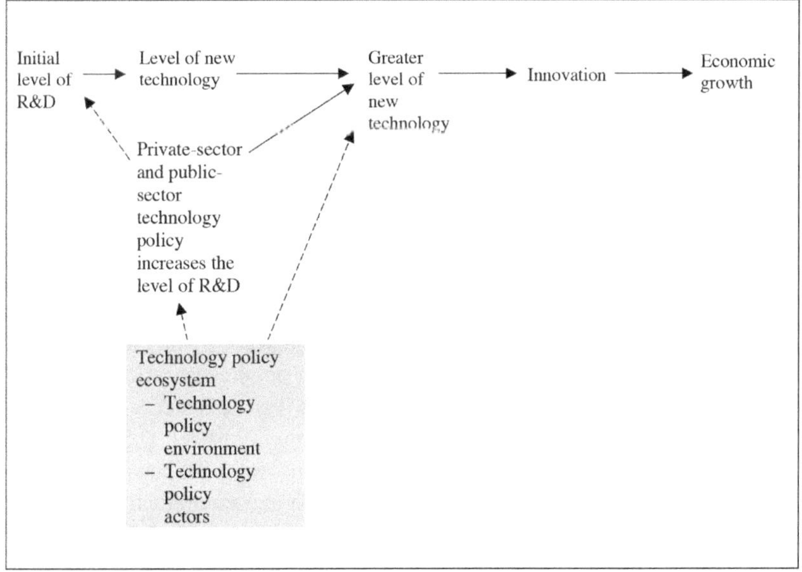

Source: Prepared by the authors.

Figure 8.2 Framework for explaining the role of investments in R&D and the role of private-sector and public-sector technology policies expanded to include the technology policy ecosystem

In this concluding chapter, we develop what we call the "Technology policy ecosystem" as noted in Figure 8.2, and we introduce into the ecosystem the actors that are fundamental in implementing the institutional infrastructures which defined the "Technology policy environment" as discussed in earlier chapters.

Thus, one answer to the question above is that countries differ in the effectiveness of their technology policies because of differences in the effectiveness of the actors who are charged with implementing those policies. With this as our answer, and with no quantitative data to support our supposition other than human capital theory, we offer the arguments in this concluding chapter as a prologue for future technology policy considerations as well as for future technology policy research.[1]

ACTORS IN A TECHNOLOGY POLICY ECOSYSTEM

In earlier chapters, and in particular in Chapter 5 and in Figure 5.1, our framework diagram included the "Technology policy environment." Our discussions there focused on an environment that contained two institutional infrastructures: a patent system and a structure that encouraged collaborative R&D. Our focus on these two so-called environmental elements was somewhat pragmatic because most countries have an established patent system and a number of countries had program or policy structures to encourage collaborative R&D.

In this chapter, we introduce three sets of actors into the ecosystem that have a direct effect on the effectiveness of a country's technology policy, and along with the two elements of a "Technology policy environment," we have constructed what we call the "Technology policy ecosystem."

We introduce this set of actors in this concluding chapter for three reasons. First, consideration of these additional actors allows us to *begin* (our emphasis) to suggest an answer to the question posed just above: Why do countries differ so much in the effectiveness of their innovation policies as reflected through the effectiveness of their technology policies (as reflected through their private-sector and public-sector levels of investment in R&D)? Second, little is known from either a policy perspective or from a research perspective about the role of these actors, but they do have, at least at a theoretical level, a conceptual result of the effectiveness of technology policy. And third, through our introduction of a "Technology policy ecosystem," we now have a pulpit from which to suggest the need for an understanding of the dynamic elements of technology policy, where the adjective *dynamic* refers to the time elements associated with the effective introduction and implementation of technology policy tools. We posit that these time-related elements are not independent of the scope of abilities of the actors and the changing size of the ecosystem.[2]

From the evidence that we have presented in the previous chapters, we are in a grounded position to suggest that countries with a distinctly defined technology policy and innovation policy have performed better from a general economic perspective than a country without both. Consequently, we suggest that countries need to give due consideration to adopting distinct technology policies that reflect more explicitly national efforts to embrace knowledge creation and exploitation in the most effective manner possible, and the actors within the "Technology policy ecosystem" are critical to achieving that objective.

The challenge of creating and implementing an effective technology policy is significant and not to be underestimated. Nevertheless, we suggest that given the changing nature and profile of economies, the development of clear technology policies can underpin policy efforts to successfully evolve economies and their structures to adequately and responsively meet the challenge posed by the creation and exploitation of new knowledge and the underlying technology that is created as a result.

There is a constellation of different actors (within three broadly defined groups) relevant to an effective technology policy as we discuss below.

Policy Instrument Creators

Policy instrument creators are those who are tasked by governments to identify the potential elements of a technology policy and to match those elements with the resource base of the country. This effort encompasses focusing on particular knowledge arenas, the legislative framework that is required to enact into law a technology policy and its various economic incentives, as well as other public investments that are necessary to support effectively a particular technology policy.

One of the most challenging aspects for policy instrument creators is defining relevant boundaries with respect to the scope of the policy vis-à-vis the resources of the country. We have highlighted in the previous chapters that technology policy can either be forward looking to focus on current or future policy needs to respond to a variety of policy demands. Such differences in approaches reflect the immediate policy demands, national ambitions, aspirations, and the resources and capability endowments within a national economy. There are different directions that policy makers can suggest to legislators for how and when to pursue policy needs as discussed in Chapter 7. Such differences are also a reflection on the legislator's appreciation and understanding of how technology policy, along with other policies like entrepreneurship policy and innovation policies, can contribute individually or synergistically to sustainable economic development and growth.

The task for policy instrument creators is a challenging and complex one. There are not only policy scope challenges to contend with, but also there are needs relevant to providing ongoing assurances to national governments that a policy intervention will achieve the desired outcomes necessary to achieve short-term and well as more medium- to long-term impacts. Moreover, there is also an increasing need for policy instrument creators to translate the technology policy intent into a legislative framework so that the policy can be scrutinized and debated at a national level. This transparency provides a legal foundation to support follow-on public investments that are necessary for current and continued implementation.

Policy Enablers

Within the sphere of public policy development and implementation, there can be an array of policy enablers that support the implementation of technology policy, such as those individuals within public funding agencies, within public research organizations, within publicly funded higher educational institutions, and within industrial development agencies. A legislative framework provides policy enablers with a clear mandate and the legitimacy and authority required to carry out the technology policy implementation. Specifically, the responsibility of implementing technology policy may lie in the hands of those who understand the interplay among economics, science, and technology. While there will be some coordination among these individuals, implementation responsibilities are nevertheless their separate mandates.

The role of those in public funding agencies typically focuses on designing appropriate research programs that mobilize scientific communities within universities, public research organizations, and those in private-sector firms to support the realization of a technology policy. Such program outcomes and impacts are difficult to predict given the predominant focus on novelty and originality that is an inherent feature of this type of activity. Only with the benefit of insight (i.e., informed perception of opportunities) can the value of such programs be measured and truly understood.

Those within public research organizations support technology policy in at least two ways. First, they take a research programmatic lead in pursuing the necessary activities in order to create new knowledge. Second, they participate in larger consortia collaborating alongside scientists at universities, private firms, or other public research organizations. When the capabilities and competencies of those within research organizations come to the fore, they become invaluable supporting actors of a technology policy.

Those within publicly funded HEIs can contribute to supporting the development and implementation of a technology policy through their intertwined missions of teaching, research, and technology and knowledge transfer.

HEI-based scientists with domain expertise can contribute to policy development and to the implementation side through leading or being members of public research programs. The technology and knowledge transfer mission of those in HEIs is effectively utilized when proprietary knowledge has been created that can be exploited by third parties through technology transfer mechanisms. The teaching mission comes to the fore as new knowledge becomes more pervasive, and there is growing demand from industry for knowledge expertise on how to enable the application of technology policy developments. In turn, HEIs are asked to respond with the development of post-graduate, undergraduate degree programs and specialized programs.

Within the public policy arena, most developed economies have policy enablers within industrial development agencies that are focused on attracting foreign direct investment (FDI) and supporting job creation and growth. Consequently, the role of such policy enablers in technology policy development is orientated toward implementation and devising support programs that will incentivize firms to adopt and exploit newly created technical knowledge.

Regulators

During the development of technology policy, regulatory concerns often arise. Due consideration at the policy development phase needs to be given to the adequacy of current intellectual property, competition, and consumer protection laws and regulations. Given unanticipated consequences, especially with respect to technology policy, governments need to ensure that the legal frameworks and regulatory regimes are not only sufficiently robust so that they do not constrain technology policy development and evolution but also sufficiently flexible so that they can provide the appropriate legal protections and remedies to all affected parties.

FINAL REFLECTIONS ON TECHNOLOGY AND INNOVATION POLICIES

One of our main motivations throughout the book has been to highlight the relevance and importance of technology policy and innovation policy to national economies and societies and along that road to emphasize the relationship between technology policy and innovation. While we have approached technology policy and innovation policy as enabling legislative initiatives focused on achieving economic growth, we are aware that we have told only one-half of the story that is related to the guiding paradigm of this book:

R&D → technology → innovation → economic growth

We have not addressed entrepreneurial policies that engender both private-sector and public-sector creativity. In the private sector, policy makers need to be more aware of how R&D investments—the target variable for technology policy—are managed with firms and how to stimulate creativity and perhaps risk taking among those individuals. In the public sector, policy makers need to be more aware of the possibilities of myriad ways to implement technology policy.[3] Hopefully, these will be topics for further consideration in the future.

NOTES

1. We have deliberately chosen the ecosystem approach because it highlights the interdependent nature of the different elements and infrastructures that affect technology policy and hence innovation policy.
2. One might interpret our charge in this chapter as a call for the integration of sociological elements into technology policy considerations, and one would be correct.
3. See Leyden and Link (2015) and Link and Link (2009) on public-sector entrepreneurship.

References

Albats, Ekaterina, Irina Fiegenbaum, and James A. Cunningham (2018). "A Micro Level Study of University Industry Collaborative Lifecycle Key Performance Indicators," *Journal of Technology Transfer*, 43: 389–431.

Andries, Petra and Dries Faems (2013). "Patenting Activities and Firm Performance: Does Firm Size Matter?" *Journal of Product Innovation Management*, 30: 1089–98.

Arrow, Kenneth, (1962). "Economic Welfare and the Allocation of Resources for Invention," in *The Rate and Direction of Inventive Activity: Economic and Social Factors* (pp. 609–25), Princeton, NJ: Princeton University Press.

Artz, Kendall W., Patricia M. Norman, and Donald E. Hatfield (2003). "Firm Performance: A Longitudinal Study of R&D, Patents and Product Innovation," *Academy of Management Proceedings*, 1: B1–B6.

Artz, Kendall W., Patricia M. Norman, Donald E. Hatfield, and Laura B. Cardinal (2010). "A Longitudinal Study of the Impact of R&D, Patents, and Product Innovation on Firm Performance," *Journal of Product Innovation Management*, 27: 725–40.

Arvanitis, Spyros (1997). "The Impact of Firm Size on Innovative Activity—an Empirical Analysis Based on Swiss Firm Data," *Small Business Economics*, 9: 473–90.

Arvanitis, Spyros (2012). "How Do Different Motives for R&D Cooperation Affect Firm Performance?—an Analysis Based on Swiss Micro Data," *Journal of Evolutionary Economics*, 22: 981–1007.

Asheim, Bjørn T. (2019). "Smart Specialisation, Innovation Policy and Regional Innovation Systems: What about New Path Development in Less Innovative Regions?" *Innovation: The European Journal of Social Science Research*, 32: 8–25.

Audretsch, David B., James A. Cunningham, Donald F. Kuratko, Erik E. Lehmann, and Metthias Menter (2019a). "Entrepreneurial Ecosystems: Economic, Technological, and Societal Impacts, *Journal of Technology Transfer*, 44: 313–25.

Audretsch, David B., Albert N. Link, and Mike Wright (2019b). "Disciplinary Perspectives on Innovation," *Foundations and Trends in Entrepreneurship*, 15: 1–172.

Autio, Erkko and Llewellyn D.W. Thomas (2014). "Innovation Ecosystems: Implications for Innovation Management," in *The Oxford Handbook of Innovation Management* (M. Dodgson, D.M. Gann, and N. Phillips, eds., pp. 204–88), Oxford: Oxford University Press.

Bach, Laurent., Mireille Matt, and Sandrine Wolff (2014). "How Do Firms Perceive Policy Rationales Behind the Variety of Instruments Supporting Collaborative R&D? Lessons from the European Framework Programs," *Technovation*, 34: 327–37.

Balasubramanian, Natarajan and Jagadeesh Sivadasan (2011). "What Happens When Firms Patent? New Evidence from US Economic Census Data," *The Review of Economics and Statistics*, 93: 126–46.

Barry, Frank (2007). "Foreign Direct Investment and Institutional Co-evolution in Ireland," *Scandinavian Economic History Review*, 55: 262–88.

Bastiat, Frédéric (1995). *Selected Essays on Political Economy*, trans. Seymour Cain, ed. George B. de Huszar, Irvington-on-Hudson: Foundation for Economic Education, originally published 1848. Available at: https://oll.libertyfund.org/titles/bastiat-selected-essays-on-political-economy (accessed July 27, 2020).

Bayona, Christina, Teresa García-Marco, and Emilio Huerta (2001). "Firms' Motivations for Cooperative R&D: An Empirical Analysis of Spanish Firms," *Research Policy*, 30: 1289–307.

Becker, Bettina (2015). "Public R&D Policies and Private R&D Investment: A Survey of the Empirical Evidence," *Journal of Economic Surveys*, 29: 917–42.

Becker, Bettina (2019). "The Impact of Innovation Policy on Firm Innovation and Performance: A Review of Recent Research Developments," *ifo DICE Report*, 17: 10–15.

Belenzon, Sharon and Andrea Patacconi (2014). "How Does Firm Size Moderate Firms' Ability to Benefit from Invention? Evidence from Patents and Scientific Publications," *European Management Review*, 11: 21–45.

Bellini, Emilio, Piroli, Giuseppe, and Luca Pennacchio (2019). "Collaborative Know-how and Trust in University–Industry Collaborations: Empirical Evidence from ICT Firms," *Journal of Technology Transfer*, 44: 1939–63.

Belussi, Fiorenza and Katia Caldari (2009). "At the Origin of the Industrial District: Alfred Marshall and the Cambridge School," *Cambridge Journal of Economics*, 33: 335–55.

Berbegal-Mirabent, Jasmina, Esteban Lafuente, and Francesc Solé (2013). "The Pursuit of Knowledge Transfer Activities: An Efficiency Analysis of Spanish Universities," *Journal of Business Research*, 66: 2051–9.

Bilbao-Osorio, Beñat and Andrés Rodríguez-Pose (2004). "From R&D to Innovation and Economic Growth in the EU," *Growth and Change*, 35: 434–55.

Birkinshaw, Julian, Gary Hamel, and Michael J. Mol (2008). "Management Innovation," *Academy of Management Review*, 33: 825–45.

Bloom, Nicholas and John Van Reenen (2002). "Patents, Real Options and Firm Performance," *The Economic Journal*, 112: C97–C116.

Bogers, Marcel (2011). "The Open Innovation Paradox: Knowledge Sharing and Protection in R&D Collaborations," *European Journal of Innovation Management*, 14: 93–117.

Bozeman, Barry and Albert N. Link (1984). "Tax Incentives for R&D: A Critical Evaluation," *Research Policy*, 13: 21–31.

Bozeman, Barry, Albert N. Link, and Asghar Zardkoohi (1986). "An Economic Analysis of R&D Joint Ventures," *Managerial and Decision Economics*, 7: 263–6.

Brankovic, Nina (2017). "Developing Entrepreneurial Universities in a Post-Communist Country: The Case of Bosnia and Herzegovina," in *Entrepreneurial Universities: Technology and Knowledge Transfer* (J. Cunningham, M. Guerrero, and D. Urbano, eds., pp. 111–63), London: World Scientific Publishers.

Brouwer, Erik and Alfred Kleinknecht (1999). "Innovative Output, and a Firm's Propensity to Patent: An Exploration of CIS Micro Data," *Research Policy*, 28: 615–24.

Brown, Ross (2016). "Mission Impossible? Entrepreneurial Universities and Peripheral Regional Innovation Systems," *Industry and Innovation*, 23: 189–205.

Bush, Vannevar (1945). *Science—the Endless Frontier*, Washington, DC: National Science Foundation.

Cantner, Uwe, James A. Cunningham, Erik E. Lehmann, and Matthias Menter (2020). "Entrepreneurial Ecosystems: A Dynamic Lifecycle Model," *Small Business Economics*, doi: 10.1007/s11187–020–00316–0.

Carayannis, Elias G. and David F.J. Campbell (2009). "'Mode 3' and 'Quadruple Helix': Toward a 21st Century Fractal Innovation Ecosystem," *International Journal of Technology Management*, 46: 201–34.

Carter, President Jimmy (1979). "Joint Hearings before the U.S. Senate Committee on Commerce, Science, and Transportation and the Select Committee on Small Business; and to the U.S. House of Representatives Committee on Science and Technology and the Committee on Small Business," Washington, DC: Government Printing Office.

Cerulli, Giovanni and Bianca Potì (2012). "The Differential Impact of Privately and Publicly Funded R&D on R&D Investment and Innovation: The Italian Case," *Prometheus*, 30: 113–49.

Chesbrough, Henry (2010). "Business Model Innovation: Opportunities and Barriers," *Long Range Planning*, 43: 354–63.

Civera, Alice, Erik E. Lehmann, Stefano Paleari, and Sarah A.E. Stockinger (2020). "Higher Education Policy: Why Hope for Quality When Rewarding Quantity?" *Research Policy*, 49: 104083.

Clark, Burton R. (1998). *Creating Entrepreneurial Universities: Organizational Pathways of Transformation*, New York: Elsevier Science.

Coenen, Lars, Teis Hansen, and Josephine V. Rekers (2015). "Innovation Policy for Grand Challenges: An Economic Geography Perspective," *Geography Compass*, 9: 483–96.

Cohen, Wesley M., Richard Florida, Lucien Randazzese, and John P. Walsh (1997). "Industry and the Academy: Uneasy Partners in the Cause of Technological Advance," in *Challenge to the University* (R. Noll, ed., pp. 171–200), Washington, DC: Brookings Institution Press.

Cornet, Maarten, Björn Vroomen, and Marc van der Steeg (2006). "Do Innovation Vouchers Help SMEs to Cross the Bridge Towards Science?" CPB Netherlands Bureau for Economic Policy Analysis Discussion Paper 58, https://www.cpb.nl/en/publication/do-innovation-vouchers-help-smes-cross-bridge-towards-science (accessed November 11, 2020).

Cunningham, James A. and William Golden (2015). "National Innovation System of Ireland," *Wiley Encyclopedia of Management, Technology and Innovation Management* vol. 13: 1–14.

Cunningham, James A. and Brian Harney (2012). *Strategy and Strategists*, Oxford: Oxford University Press.

Cunningham, James A. and Albert N. Link (2015). "Fostering University-Industry R&D Collaborations in European Union Countries," *International Entrepreneurship and Management Journal*, 11: 849–60.

Cunningham, James A. and Albert N. Link (2016). "Exploring the Effectiveness of Research and Innovation Policies among European Union Countries," *International Entrepreneurship and Management Journal*, 12: 415–25.

Cunningham, James A. and Matthias Menter (2020a). "Micro-Level Academic Entrepreneurship: A Research Agenda," *Journal of Management Development*, doi: 10.1108/JMD-04–2020–0129.

Cunningham, James A. and Matthias Menter (2020b). "Transformative Change in Higher Education: Entrepreneurial Universities and High-Technology Entrepreneurship," *Industry and Innovation*, doi:10.1080/13662716.2020.1763263.

Cunningham, James A. and Grace S. Walsh (2019). "Disciplinary Perspectives on Innovation: Management," *Foundations and Trends® in Entrepreneurship*, 15: 391–430.

Cunningham, James A., Paul O'Reilly, Conor O'Kane, and Vincent Mangematin (2016). "Publicly Funded Principal Investigators as Transformative Agents of Public Sector Entrepreneurship," in *Essays in Public Sector Entrepreneurship* (D. Audretsch and A. Link, eds., pp. 67–94), New York: Springer.

Cunningham, James A., Erik E. Lehmann, Matthias Menter, and Nikolaus Seitz. (2019a). "The Impact of University Focused Technology Transfer Policies on Regional Innovation and Entrepreneurship," *Journal of Technology Transfer*, 44: 1451–75.

Cunningham, James A., Matthias Menter, and Katharine Wirsching (2019b). "Entrepreneurial Ecosystem Governance: A Principal Investigator-Centered Governance Framework," *Small Business Economics*, 52: 545–62.

Cunningham, James A., Paul O'Reilly, Daire Hooper, Daniel Nepelski, and Vincent Van Roy (2020). "The Role of Project Coordinators in European Commission Framework Programme Projects. Results of the Innovation Radar PC Survey in FPR&I Projects," EUR 30131 EN, Luxembourg: Publication Office of the European Union, ISBN 978–92–76–17304–5, doi:10.2760/709126, JRC120015.

Darroch, Jenny (2005). "Knowledge Management, Innovation and Firm Performance," *Journal of Knowledge Management*, 9: 101–15.

Dasgupta, Partha and Paul Stoneman, (2005). *Economic Policy and Technological Performance*, Cambridge: Cambridge University Press.

Davey, Todd and Victoria Galan-Muros (2020). "Understanding Entrepreneurial Academics: How They Perceive Their Environment Differently," *Journal of Management Development*, doi: 10.1108/JMD-09–2019–0392.

David, Paul A., Bronwyn H. Hall, and Andrew A. Toole (2000). "Is Public R&D a Complement or Substitute for Private R&D? A Review of the Econometric Evidence," *Research Policy*, 29: 497–529.

Doh, Jonathan P., Thomas C. Lawton, and Tazeeb Rajwani (2012). "Advancing Nonmarket Strategy Research: Institutional Perspectives in a Changing World," *Academy of Management Perspectives*, 26: 22–39.

Dolan, Brendan, James A. Cunningham, Metthias Menter, and Caroline McGregor (2019). "The Role and Function of Cooperative Research Centers in Entrepreneurial Universities," *Management Decision*, 57: 3406–25.

Dolfsma, Wilfred (2011). "Government Failure—Four Types," *Journal of Economic Issues*, 3: 593–604.

Dowling, Ann (2015). *The Dowling Review of Business-University Research Collaborations*, https://www.raeng.org.uk/publications/reports/the-dowling-review-of-business-university-research (accessed November 8, 2020).

Duchêne, Vincent, Elissuvet Lykogianni, and Arnold Verbeek (2011). "The EU R&D Under-investment: Patterns in R&D Expenditure and Financing," *European Science and Technology Policy: Towards Integration or Fragmentation?* 193.

EC (European Commission) (2008). *Regional Research Intensive Clusters and Science Parks*, Luxembourg: Publication Office of the European Union.

EC (European Commission) (2017a). *R&D Tax Incentives: How to Make Them Most Effective?* Luxembourg: Publication Office of the European Union.

EC (European Commission) (2017b). *Regional Research Intensive Clusters and Science Parks*, Brussels: Publication Office of the European Union.

EC (European Commission) (2018). *Proposal for a Regulation of the European Parliament and of the Council Establishing Horizon Europe—the Framework Programme for Research and Innovation*, Brussels: Publication Office of the European Union.

EC (European Commission) (2020). *Knowledge Transfer Metrics: Towards a European-Wide Set of Harmonized Indictors*, Seville, Spain: Joint Research Centre, https://ec.europa.eu/growth/industry/policy/innovation_en.

EPO (European Patent Office) (2020a). "Welcome to the Patent Index 2019," https://www.epo.org/about-us/annual-reports-statistics/statistics/2019.html (accessed November 2, 2020).

EPO (European Patent Office) (2020b). "Patent Index 2019: Statistics at a Glance," http://documents.epo.org/projects/babylon/eponet.nsf/0/BC45C92E5C077B10C1258527004E95C0/$File/Patent_Index_2019_statistics_at_a_glance_en.pdf (accessed November 2, 2020).

Esmaeilpoorarabi, Niusha, Tan Yigitcanlar, and Mirko Guaralda (2018). "Place Quality in Innovation Clusters: An Empirical Analysis of Global Best Practices from Singapore, Helsinki, New York, and Sydney," *Cities*, 74: 156–68.

Fagerberg, Jan (2017). "Innovation Policy: Rationales, Lessons and Challenges," *Journal of Economic Surveys*, 31: 497–512.

Feldman, Maryann, Johanna Francis, and Janet Bercovitz (2005). "Creating a Cluster While Building a Firm: Entrepreneurs and the Formation of Industrial Clusters," *Regional Studies*, 39: 129–41.

Fini, Ricardo, Einar Rasmussen, Donald Siegel, and Johan Wiklund (2018). "Rethinking the Commercialization of Public Science: From Entrepreneurial Outcomes to Societal Impacts," *Academy of Management Perspectives*, 32: 4–20.

Fisher, Erik (2005). "Lessons Learned from the Ethical, Legal and Social Implications Program (ELSI): Planning Societal Implications Research for the National Nanotechnology Program," *Technology in Society*, 27: 321–8.

Flanagan, Kieron, Elvira Uyarra, and Manuel Laranja (2011). "Reconceptualising the 'Policy Mix' for Innovation," *Research Policy*, 40: 702–13.

Freeman, Chris (2002). "Continental, National and Sub-national Innovation Systems—Complementarity and Economic Growth," *Research Policy*, 31: 191–211.

Frumkin, Maximilian (1945). "The Origin of Patents," *Journal of the Patent Office Society*, 27: 143–8.

Gertner, Drew, Joanne Roberts, and David Charles (2011). "University-Industry Collaboration: A CoPs Approach to KTPs," *Journal of Knowledge Management*, 15: 625–47.

Gingrich, Nicole, Michael Hall, and Isaac Patterson (2020). "An Initial Look at Federal Offices of Research and Technology Applications," *Journal of Research of the National Institute of Standards and Technology*, 125: 125033–49.

Giuri, Paola, Federico Munari, Alessandra Scandura, and Laura Toschi (2019). "The Strategic Orientation of Universities in Knowledge Transfer Activities," *Technological Forecasting and Social Change*, 138: 261–78.

Godin, Benoît (2006). "The Linear Model of Innovation: The Historical Construction of an Analytical Framework," *Science, Technology, and Human Values*, 31: 639–67.

Goel, Rajeev K., Devrim Göktepe-Hultén, and Christoph Grimpe (2017). "Who Instigates University–Industry Collaborations? University Scientists versus Firm Employees," *Small Business Economics*, 48: 503–24.

González, Xulia and Consuelo Pazó (2008). "Do Public Subsidies Stimulate Private R&D Spending?" *Research Policy*, 37: 371–89.

Gores, Thorsten and Albert N. Link (2021). "The Globalization of the Bayh-Dole Act," *Annals of Science and Technology Policy*, 5: 1–90.

Görg, Holger and Eric Strobl (2007). "The Effect of R&D Subsidies on Private R&D," *Economica*, 74: 215–34.

Green, Roy, James Cunningham, Imelda Duggan, Majella Giblin, Mike Moroney, and Leo Smyth (2001). "The Boundaryless Cluster: Information and Communications Technology in Ireland," in *Innovative Clusters Drivers of National Innovation Systems* (pp. 47–64), Paris: OECD.

Griliches, Zvi (1986). "Productivity, R and D, and Basic Research at the Firm Level in the 1970's," *American Economic Review*, 76: 141–54.

Grimes, Seamus and Patrick Collins (2009). "The Contribution of the Overseas ICT Sector to Expanding R&D Investment in Ireland," *Irish Geography*, 42: 45–67.

GTIPA (Global Trade and Innovation Policy Alliance) (2019). *National Innovation Policies: What Countries Do Best and How They Can Improve*, Washington, DC: Global Trade and Innovation Policy Alliance.

Guellec, Dominique and Bruno van Pottelsberghe de la Potterie (2001). "R&D and Productivity Growth: Panel Data Analysis of 16 OECD Countries," *OECD Economic Studies*, 33: 103–26.

Guerrero, Maribel, David Urbano, James A. Cunningham, and D. Organ (2014). "Entrepreneurial Universities in Two European Regions: A Case Study Comparison," *Journal of Technology Transfer*, 39: 415–34.

Guinet, Jean and Hiroko Kamata (1996). "Do Tax-Incentives Promote Innovation?" *OECD Observer*, 202: 22.

Hall, Bronwyn H. and Rosemarie H. Ziedonis (2001). "The Patent Paradox Revisited: An Empirical Study of Patenting in the US Semiconductor Industry, 1979–1995," *Rand Journal of Economics*, 32: 101–28.

Hall, Bronwyn H., Jacques Mairesse, and Pierre Mohnen (2010). "Measuring the Returns to R&D," in *Economics of Innovation* (B. Hall and N. Rosenberg, eds., pp. 1034–82), Amsterdam: North-Holland.

Hall, C. Michael (2009). "Innovation and Tourism Policy in Australia and New Zealand: Never the Twain Shall Meet?" *Journal of Policy Research in Tourism, Leisure and Events*, 1: 2–18.

Harvey, Kerron (1992). "Managing the Exploitation of Intellectual Property: An Analysis of Policy and Practice in Nine UK Universities," Doctor of Philosophy thesis at the University of Stirling, U.K.

Hayter, Christopher S., Albert N. Link, and John T. Scott (2018). "Public-Sector Entrepreneurship," *Oxford Review of Economic Policy*, 34: 676–94.

Hayter, Christopher S. and Albert N. Link (2020). "Governance Mechanisms Enabling Interorganizational Adaptation: Lessons from Grand Challenge R&D Programs," *Science and Public Policy*, 47: 271–82.

Hébert, Robert F. and Albert N. Link (2009). *A History of Entrepreneurship*, New York: Routledge.

Hertzfeld, Henry R., Albert N. Link, and Nicholas S. Vonortas (2006). "Intellectual Property Protection Mechanisms in Research Partnerships," *Research Policy*, 35: 82538.

HESA (2017). Higher Education Business and Community Interaction Survey, 2015/16, https://www.hesa.ac.uk/data-and-analysis/publications/hebci-2015–16 (accessed October 18, 2020).

Hewitt-Dundas, Nola (2012). "Research Intensity and Knowledge Transfer Activity in UK Universities," *Research Policy*, 41: 262–75.

Hilliard, Rachel and Roy Green (2005). "Governance and Institutional Change in Ireland," *Governance of Innovation Systems*, 2: 43–64.
Hobbs, Kelsi G., Albert N. Link, and John T. Scott (2017). "Science and Technology Parks: An Annotated and Analytical Literature Review," *Journal of Technology Transfer*, 42: 957–76.
Hobbs, Kelsi G., Albert N. Link, and Terri L. Shelton (2020). "The Regional Economic Impacts of University Research and Science Parks," *Journal of the Knowledge Economy*, 11: 42–56.
Hong, Jae-pyo (2017). "Causal Relationship between ICT R&D Investment and Economic Growth in Korea," *Technological Forecasting and Social Change*, 116: 70–5.
Hottenrott, Hanna and Sascha Rexhäuser (2015). "Policy-Induced Environmental Technology and Inventive Efforts: Is There a Crowding Out?" *Industry and Innovation*, 22: 375–401.
Hu, Albert G. (2001). "Ownership, Government R&D, Private R&D, and Productivity in Chinese Industry," *Journal of Comparative Economics*, 29: 136–57.
Hussinger, Katrin (2006). "Is Silence Golden? Patents Versus Secrecy at the Firm Level," *Economics of Innovation and New Technology*, 15: 735–52.
Iammarino, Simona and Phillip McCann (2006). "The Structure and Evolution of Industrial Clusters: Transactions, Technology and Knowledge Spillovers," *Research Policy*, 35: 1018–36.
Jones, Shannon E. and Nigel Coates (2020). "A Micro-Level View on Knowledge Co-creation through University-Industry Collaboration in a Multi-National Corporation," *Journal of Management Development*, doi:10.1108/JMD-08-2019-0365.
Kafouros, Mario I. (2005). "R&D and Productivity Growth: Evidence from the UK," *Economics of Innovation and New Technology*, 14: 479–97.
Katz, Bruce and Julie Wagner (2014). "The Rise of Innovation Districts: A New Geography of Innovation in America," https://www.brookings.edu/essay/rise-of-innovation-districts/ (accessed November 11, 2020).
Khan, B. Zorina (undated). "An Economic History of Patent Institutions," https://web.archive.org/web/20060502201648/http://eh.net/encyclopedia/article/khan.patents (accessed July 21, 2020).
Khan, B. Zorina and Kenneth L. Sokoloff (2004). "Institutions and Technological Innovation during the Early Economic Growth: Evidence from the Great Inventors of the United States, 1790–1930," National Bureau of Economic Research Working Paper 10966.
Kim, Sun G. (2000). "Is Government Investment in R&D and Market Environment Needed for Indigenous Private R&D in Less Developed Countries? Evidence from Korea," *Science and Public Policy*, 27: 13–22.
Kirby, David A. (2006). "Creating Entrepreneurial Universities in the UK: Applying Entrepreneurship Theory to Practice," *Journal of Technology Transfer*, 31: 599–603.
Kuhlmann, Stefan (2001). "Future Governance of Innovation Policy in Europe—Three Scenarios," *Research Policy*, 30: 953–76.
Kwong, Matt (2014). "Six Significant Moments in Patent History," https://www.reuters.com/article/us-moments-patent-idUSKBN0IN1Y120141104 (accessed July 21, 2020).
Le Grand, Julian (1991). "The Theory of Government Failure," *British Journal of Political Science*, 21: 423–42.

Lehmann, Erik E. and Sarah A.E. Stockinger (2019). "Entrepreneurship in Higher Education: The Impact of Competition-Based Policy Programmes Exemplified by the German Excellence Initiative," *Higher Education Quarterly*, 73: 70–84.

Leyden, Dennis Patrick and Albert N. Link (1993). "Tax Policies Affecting R&D: An International Comparison," *Technovation*, 13: 17–25.

Leyden, Dennis Patrick and Albert N. Link (2015). *Public Sector Entrepreneurship: U.S. Technology and Innovation Policy*, New York: Oxford University Press.

Leydesdorff, Loet and Henry Etzkowitz (1998). "The Triple Helix as a Model for Innovation Studies," *Science and Public Policy*, 25: 195–203.

Leydesdorff, Loet and Martin Meyer (2003). "The Triple Helix of University-Industry-Government Relations," *Scientometrics*, 58: 191–203.

Lichtenberg, Frank R. (1992). "R&D Investment and International Productivity Differences," NBER Working Papers 4161, National Bureau of Economic Research.

Lichtenberg, Frank R. and Donald S. Siegel (1991). "The Impact of R&D Investment on Productivity: New Evidence Using Linked R&D–LRD Data," *Economic Inquiry*, 29: 203–29.

Link, Albert N. (1981). "Basic Research and Productivity Increase in Manufacturing: Additional Evidence," *American Economic Review*, 71: 1111–12.

Link, Albert N. (1993). "Methods for Evaluating the Return on R&D Investments," in *Evaluating R&D Impacts: Methods and Practice* (pp. 1–16), Boston, MA: Springer.

Link, Albert N. (2006). *Public/Private Partnerships: Innovation Strategies and Policy Alternatives*, New York: Springer.

Link, Albert N. (2013). *Public Support of Innovation in Entrepreneurial Firms*, Cheltenham, UK and Northampton, MA, USA: Edward Elgar.

Link, Albert N. (2020a). *Collaborative Research in the United States: Policies and Institutions for Cooperation among Firms*, New York: Routledge.

Link, Albert N. (2020b). "University Science and Technology Parks: A U.S. Perspective," in *Science and Technology Parks and Regional Economic Development: An International Perspective* (S. Amoroso, A. Link, and M. Wright, eds., pp. 25–38), New York: Palgrave Macmillan.

Link, Albert N. (2021a). *Collaborative R&D and the National Research Joint Venture Database: A Statistical Analysis*, New York: Emerald Group Publishing.

Link, Albert N. (2021b). *Invention, Innovation, and U.S. Federal Laboratories*, Cheltenham, UK and Northampton, MA, USA: Edward Elgar.

Link, Albert N. and Laura L. Bauer (1989). *Cooperative Research in U.S. Manufacturing: Assessing Policy Initiatives and Corporate Strategies*, Lexington, MA: D.C. Heath.

Link, Albert N. and James A. Cunningham (2021). *Advanced Introduction to Technology Policy*, Cheltenham, UK and Northampton, MA, USA: Edward Elgar.

Link, Albert N. and Jamie R. Link (2009). *Government as Entrepreneur*, New York: Oxford University Press.

Link, Albert N. and Zachary T. Oliver (2020). *Technology Transfer and U.S. Public Sector Innovation*, Cheltenham, UK and Northampton, MA, USA: Edward Elgar.

Link, Albert N. and John T. Scott (2001). "Public/Private Partnerships: Stimulating Competition in a Dynamic Market," *International Journal of Industrial Organization*, 19: 763–94.

Link, Albert N. and John T. Scott (2006). "U.S. University Research Parks," *Journal of Productivity Analysis*, 25: 43–55.

Link, Albert N. and John T. Scott (2007). "The Economics of University Research Parks," *Oxford Review of Economic Policy*, 23: 661–74.

Link, Albert N. and John T. Scott (2011). *Public Goods, Public Gains: Calculating the Social Benefits of Public R&D*, New York: Oxford University Press.

Link, Albert N. and John T. Scott (2012). "Employment Growth from Public Support of Innovation in Small Firms," *Economics of Innovation and New Technology*, 21, 655–78.

Link, Albert N. and John T. Scott (2018). "Geographic Proximity and Science Parks," in *Oxford Research Encyclopedia of Economics and Finance*, doi:10.1093/acrefore/9780190625979.013.272.

Link, Albert N. and Martijn van Hasselt (2019). "On the Transfer of Technology from Universities: The Impact of the Bayh–Dole Act of 1980 on the Institutionalization of University Research," *European Economic Review*, 119: 472–81.

Link, Albert N. and Martijn van Hasselt (2020). "The Use of Intellectual Property Protection Mechanisms by Publicly Supported Firms," *Economics of Innovation and New Technology*, doi: 10.1080/10438599.2020.1843993.

Link, Albert N. and Charles W. Wessner (2011). "Universities as Research Partners: Entrepreneurial Explorations and Exploitations," in *Handbook of Research on Innovation and Entrepreneurship* (D. Audretsch, ed., pp. 290–2), Cheltenham, UK and Northampton, MA, USA: Edward Elgar.

Lokshin, Boris and Pierre Mohnen (2012). "How Effective Are Level-Based R&D Tax Credits? Evidence from the Netherlands," *Applied Economics*, 44: 1527–38.

Lundvall, Bengt-Åke (2007). "National Innovation Systems—Analytical Concept and Development Tool," *Industry and Innovation*, 14: 95–119.

Manchester Institute of Innovation Research (2015). *A Review of the Small Business Research Initiative: Final Report*, Manchester: Manchester Institute of Innovation Research, https://assets.publishing.service.gov.uk/government/uploads/system/uploads/attachment_data/file/662657/A_Review_of_the_Small_Business_Research_Initiative_.pdf.

Mangematin, Vincent, Paul O'Reilly, and James A. Cunningham (2014). "PIs as Boundary Spanners, Science and Market Shapers," *The Journal of Technology Transfer*, 39: 1–10.

Mansfield, Edwin (1968). *Industrial Research and Technological Innovation*, New York: W.W. Norton.

Mansfield, Edwin (1980). "Basic Research and Productivity Increase in Manufacturing," *American Economic Review*, 70: 863–73.

Margolis, Robert M. and Daniel M. Kammen (1999). "Evidence of Under-investment in Energy R&D in the United States and the Impact of Federal Policy," *Energy Policy*, 27: 575–84.

Marino, Marianna, Stephane Lhuillery, Pierpaolo Parrotta, and Davide Sala (2016). "Additionality or Crowding-out? An Overall Evaluation of Public R&D Subsidy on Private R&D Expenditure," *Research Policy*, 45: 1715–30.

Marshall, Alfred (1919). *Industry and Trade*, London: Macmillan.

Mazzoleni, Roberto and Richard R. Nelson (1998). "The Benefits and Costs of Strong Patent Protection: A Contribution to the Current Debate," *Research Policy*, 27: 273–84.

Mazzucato, Mariana (2017). "Mission-Oriented Innovation Policy," UCL Institute for Innovation and Public Purpose Working Paper.

Mazzucato, Mariana, Rainer Kattel, and Josh Ryan-Collins (2020). "Challenge-Driven Innovation Policy: Towards a New Policy Toolkit," *Journal of Industry, Competition and Trade*, 20: 421–37.

Meissner, Dirk, Wolfgang Polt, and Nicholas S. Vonortas (2017). "Towards a Broad Understanding of Innovation and Its Importance for Innovation Policy," *Journal of Technology Transfer*, 42: 1184–211.

Menter, Matthias, Erik Lehmann, and Torben Klarl (2018). "In Search of Excellence: A Case Study of the First Excellence Initiative of Germany," *Journal of Business Economics*, 88: 1105–32.

Merton, Robert K. (1936). "The Unanticipated Consequences of Purposive Social Action," *American Sociological Review*, 1: 894–904.

Metcalfe, John S. (1994). "Evolutionary Economics and Technology Policy," *The Economic Journal*, 104: 931–44.

Miller, Kristel, Rodney McAdam, Sandra Moffett, Allen Alexander, and Pushyarag Puthusserry (2016). "Knowledge Transfer in University Quadruple Helix Ecosystems: An Absorptive Capacity Perspective," *R&D Management*, 46: 383–99

Miller, Kristel, Allen Alexander, James A. Cunningham, and Ekaterina Albats (2018). "Entrepreneurial Academics and Academic Entrepreneurs: A Systematic Literature Review," *International Journal of Technology Management*, 77: 9–37.

Minasian, Jora R. (1969). "Research and Development, Production Functions and Rates of Return," *American Economic Review*, 59: 80–5.

Moncada-Paternò-Castello, Pietro, Constantin Ciupagea, Keith Smith, Alexander Tübke, and Mike Tubbs (2010). "Does Europe Perform Too Little Corporate R&D? A Comparison of EU and Non-EU Corporate R&D Performance," *Research Policy*, 39: 523–36.

Mothe, Caroline and Bertrand Quélin (2000). "Creating Competencies through Collaboration: The Case of EUREKA R&D Consortia," *European Management Journal*, 18: 590–604.

Motohashi, Kazuyuki (2005). "University–Industry Collaborations in Japan: The Role of New Technology-Based Firms in Transforming the National Innovation System," *Research Policy*, 34: 583–94.

Mowery, David C. (1983). "Economic Theory and Government Technology Policy," *Policy Sciences*, 16: 27–43.

Mulgan, Geoff (2019). "Innovation Districts: How Cities Speed Up the Circulation of Ideas," https://www.nesta.org.uk/blog/innovation-districts/ (accessed November 12, 2020).

Naseem, Anwar, David J. Spielman, and Steven W. Omamo (2010). "Private-Sector Investment in R&D: A Review of Policy Options to Promote Its Growth in Developing-Country Agriculture," *Agribusiness*, 26: 143–73.

Nemet, Gregory F. and Daniel M. Kammen (2007). "US Energy Research and Development: Declining Investment, Increasing Need, and the Feasibility of Expansion," *Energy Policy*, 35: 746–55.

Nepelski, Daniel and Vincent van Roy (2020). "Innovation and Innovator Assessment in R&I Ecosystems: The Case of the EU Framework Programme," *Journal of Technology Transfer*, 1–36.

Nepelski, Daniel, Vincent van Roy, and Annarosa Pesole (2019). "The Organisational and Geographic Diversity and Innovation Potential of EU-Funded Research Networks," *Journal of Technology Transfer*, 44: 359–80.

Nesta (2008). *How Inclusive Is Innovation Policy? Insights from an International Comparison*, London: Nesta.

Ng, Wei K.B., Rianne Appel-Meulenbroek, Myriam Cloodt, and Theo Arentze (2019). "Towards a Segmentation of Science Parks: A Typology Study on Science Parks in Europe," *Research Policy*, 48: 719–32.

Nkusi, Alain C., James A. Cunningham, Richard Nyuur, and Steven Pattinson (2020). "The Role of the Entrepreneurial University in Building an Entrepreneurial Ecosystem in a Post Conflict Economy: An Exploratory Study of Rwanda," *Thunderbird International Business Review*, 62: 549–63.

Norberg-Bohm, Vicki (2000). "Creating Incentives for Environmentally Enhancing Technological Change: Lessons from 30 Years of US Energy Technology Policy," *Technological Forecasting and Social Change*, 65: 125–48.

NRC (U.S. National Research Council) (2014). *Capturing Change in Science, Technology, and Innovation: Improving Indicators to Inform Policy*, Washington, DC: National Academy Press.

O'Reilly, Paul and James A. Cunningham (2017). "Enablers and Barriers to University Technology Transfer Engagements with Small- and Medium-Sized Enterprises: Perspectives of Principal Investigators," *Small Enterprise Research*, 24: 274–89.

OECD (Organisation for Economic Co-operation and Development) (*Year*). *OECD Reviews of Innovation Policy: (Country)*, Paris: OECD.

OECD (Organisation for Economic Co-operation and Development) (2015a). *Innovation Strategy 2015: An Agenda for Policy Action*, Paris: OECD.

OECD (Organisation for Economic Co-operation and Development (2015b). *The Innovation Imperative Contributing to Productivity, Growth and Well-being*, Paris: OECD.

OECD (Organisation for Economic Co-operation and Development) (2018a). *OECD Review of National R&D Tax Incentives and Estimates of R&D Tax Subsidy Rates, 2017*, Paris: OECD.

OECD (Organisation for Economic Co-operation and Development) (2018b). *The Measurement of Scientific, Technological and Innovation Activities: Oslo Manual 2018 GUIDELINES FOR COLLECTING, REPORTING AND USING DATA ON INNOVATION*, Paris: OECD.

OECD (Organisation for Economic Co-operation and Development) (2019). *OECD Compendium of Information on R&D Tax Incentives, 2919*, Paris: OECD.

OECD (Organisation for Economic Co-operation and Development) (2020). *OECD R&D Tax Incentive Database*, Paris: OECD.

Oh, Deog-Seong, Fred Phillips, Sehee Park, and Eunghyun Lee (2016). "Innovation Ecosystems: A Critical Examination," *Technovation*, 54: 1–6.

OSTP (Office of Science and Technology Policy) (1990). *U.S. Technology Policy*, Washington, DC: Executive Office of the President.

Phan, Phillip H., Donald S. Siegel, and Mike Wright (2005). "Science Parks and Incubators: Observations, Synthesis and Future Research," *Journal of Business Venturing*, 20: 165–82.

Piazza, Alessandro and Eric Abrahamson (2020). "Fads and Fashions in Management Practices: Taking Stock and Looking Forward," *International Journal of Management Reviews*, doi: 10.1111/ijmr.12225.

Roper, Stephen. (2008). "Innovation Voucher Schemes (The Netherlands, West Midlands UK, Ireland)," in *A Review of Local Economic and Employment Development Policy Approaches in OECD Countries* (pp 212–22, Paris: OECD.

Sala, Alessandro, Paolo Landoni, and Roberto Verganti (2016). "Small and Medium Enterprises Collaborations with Knowledge Intensive Services: An Explorative Analysis of the Impact of Innovation Vouchers," *R&D Management*, 46: 291–302.

Schillo, R. Sandra and Jeffrey S. Kinder (2017). "Delivering on Societal Impacts through Open Innovation: A Framework for Government Laboratories," *Journal of Technology Transfer*, 42: 977–96.

Schumpeter, Joseph A. (1928). "The Instability of Capitalism," *Economic Journal*, 38: 361–86.

Schumpeter, Joseph A. (1939). *Business Cycles*, New York: McGraw Hill.

Smyth, D.J., J.M. Samuels, and J. Tzoannos (1972). "Patents, Profitability, Liquidity and Firm Size," *Applied Economics*, 4: 77–86.

Soete, Luc (2007). "From Industrial to Innovation Policy," *Journal of Industry, Competition and Trade*, 7: 273–84.

Soh, Pek-Hooi and Annapoornima M. Subramanian (2014). "When Do Firms Benefit from University–Industry R&D Collaborations? The Implications of Firm R&D Focus on Scientific Research and Technological Recombination." *Journal of Business Venturing*, 29: 807–21.

Spigel, Ben (2017). "The Relational Organization of Entrepreneurial Ecosystems," *Entrepreneurship Theory and Practice*, 41: 49–72.

Spigel, Ben and Richard Harrison (2018). "Toward a Process Theory of Entrepreneurial Ecosystems," *Strategic Entrepreneurship Journal*, 12: 151–68.

Starbuck, Elizabeth (2001). "Optimizing University Research Collaborations," *Research-Technology Management*, 44: 40–4.

Suh, Yongyoon, Chulwan Woo, Jinhwan Koh, and Jeonghwan Jeon (2019). "Analysing the Satisfaction of University–Industry Cooperation Efforts Based on the Kano Model: A Korean Case," *Technological Forecasting and Social Change*, 148: 119740.

Tang, Mingfeng, Grace Walsh, Daniel Lerner, D., Markus A. Fitza, and Qiaohua Li (2018). "Green Innovation, Managerial Concern and Firm Performance: An Empirical Study," *Business Strategy and the Environment*, 27: 39–51.

Tassey, Gregory (2004). "Underinvestment in Public Good Technologies," *Journal of Technology Transfer*, 30: 89–113.

Tassey, Gregory (2017). "The Roles and Impacts of Technical Standards on Economic Growth and Implications for Innovation Policy," *Annals of Science and Technology Policy*, 3: 215–316.

Tassey, Gregory (2019). "Regional Technology-Based Economic Development: Policies and Impacts in the U.S. and Other Economies," *Annals of Science and Technology Policy*, 3: 1–141.

Terleckyj, Nestor E. (1974). *Effects of R&D on the Productivity Growth of Industries: An Exploratory Study*, Washington, DC: National Planning Association.

Tredgett, E.A. and Alex Coad (2014). "The Shaky Start of the UK Small Business Research Initiative (SBRI) in Comparison to the US Small Business Innovation Research Programme (SBIR)," http://papers.ssrn.com/sol3/papers.cfm?abstract_id=2205156 (accessed October 16, 2020).

Tsai, Kuen-Hung (2005). "R&D Productivity and Firm Size: A Nonlinear Examination," *Technovation*, 25: 795–803.

Tsai, Kuen-Hung and Jiann-Chyuan Wang (2004). "The Relative Impact of Government and Private R&D on Productivity Growth: A Quantitative Analysis," *International Journal of Technology, Policy and Management*, 4: 210-217.

Turner, Donald F. (1966). "Patents, Antitrust and Innovation," *University of Pittsburgh Law Review*, 28: 151–60.

Un, C. Annique and Kazuhiro Asakawa (2015). "Types of R&D Collaborations and Process Innovation: The Benefit of Collaborating Upstream in the Knowledge Chain," *Journal of Product Innovation Management*, 32: 138–53.

USDOJ (U.S. Department of Justice) (1980). *Antitrust Guide Concerning Research Joint Ventures*, Washington, DC: U.S. Department of Justice.

Valentin, Eva Maria Mora (2000). "University–Industry Cooperation: A Framework of Benefits and Obstacles," *Industry and Higher Education*, 14: 165–72.

Vick, Thais E. and Maxine Robertson (2018). "A Systematic Literature Review of UK University–Industry Collaboration for Knowledge Transfer: A Future Research Agenda," *Science and Public Policy*, 45: 579–90.

Wadho, Waqar and Azam Chaudhry (2018). "Innovation and Firm Performance in Developing Countries: The Case of Pakistani Textile and Apparel Manufacturers," *Research Policy*, 47: 1283–94.

Walrave, Bob, Madis Talmar, Ksenia S. Podoynitsyna, Georges Romme, and Geert Verbong (2018). "A Multi-Level Perspective on Innovation Ecosystems for Path-breaking Innovation," *Technological Forecasting and Social Change*, 136: 103–13.

Wang, Delu, Dylan Sutherland, Lutao Ning, Yuanoi Wang, and Xin Pan (2018). "Exploring the Influence of Political Connections and Managerial Overconfidence on R&D Intensity in China's Large-Scale Private Sector Firms," *Technovation*, 69: 40–53.

Wolf, Charles Jr. (1988). *Markets or Governments—Choosing between Imperfect Alternatives*, Cambridge, MA: MIT Press.

Wu, W. (2007). "Building Research Universities for Knowledge Transfer," in *How Universities Promote Economic Growth* (S. Yusuf and K. Nabeshima, eds., pp. 185–208), Washington, DC: The World Bank.

Xiao, Zhihua and Murray E. Fulton (2018). "Underinvestment in Producer-Funded Agricultural R&D: The Role of the Horizon Problem," *Canadian Journal of Agricultural Economics*, 66: 55–86.

Zahra, Shaker A. and Jeffrey G. Covin (1993). "Business Strategy, Technology Policy and Firm Performance," *Strategic Management Journal*, 14: 451–78.

Index

absorptive capacity 94
additionality 31, 35
Antitrust Guide Concerning Research Joint Ventures 90
asset scarcity 85

Bastiat, Frédéric 52, 53
Bayh-Dole Act (1980) 95, 96, 106, 111–14, 115

capability endowments 129
Carter, President Jimmy 56, 57, 90
collaboration
  barriers to 95, 105, 106
  in innovation 87, 88, 89, 90
  R&D 12, 43, 84–91
  science and research parks 107, 108–9, 110
  university with firm 84, 95, 102–6
creativity 73, 132
crowding out effect 35

demand-side incentives 94
dependent variable 50
depreciation allowance 38

economic growth 6, 7, 8, 9, 11, 15, 16, 24, 26, 43, 45, 53, 93, 122
  policy paradigm, in the 11, 15, 24, 45, 46, 53, 75, 124, 131
economic return 16, 26, 95
entrepreneurial ecosystems 1, 8
entrepreneurship policy 129, 132
ERDF (European Regional Development Fund) 5
EU (European Union) 4, 5, 28, 124
  European Framework Programmes 5, 6, 86, 94
  European Structural Programs 85
  tax incentives 31, 32–4

European Commission (EC) 4, 31, 103, 107, 115
European Innovation Scorecard 5
European Institute of Innovation Technology 6
European Research Area Net 6
expenditure credit 38

FDI (foreign direct investment) 131
firm-level productivity 16, 26
funding 30, 40, 58, 66, 85, 86, 105
  agencies 57, 60, 66, 67, 68, 71, 85, 130
  international sector 21
  private sector 21
  SBIR 57, 59, 60, 66, 71
  schemes 85

GDP (Gross Domestic Product) 35, 36, 38, 48, 49, 50, 120
  G7 countries 11
  Implicit Price Deflator 65
  U.K. 9, 10, 11, 30
  U.S. 9, 10, 11, 30
Global Trade and Innovation Policy Alliance 3, 8
government support 35, 36, 38, 39, 48, 49, 120

human capital 29, 128

independent variable 46, 50
industrial clusters 8
industrial policy 7
innovation
  characteristics 125
  clusters 110, 111
  collaboration in 87, 88, 89, 90
  consequence of technology policy 53
  definition 2, 3, 4, 90
  development 31

districts 110, 111
economic growth 9, 11
ecosystems 8, 127
policy paradigm, in the 11, 15, 24, 45, 53, 75, 124, 131
regional 5, 7
strategy 4, 84
systems 8, 118–22, 123
innovation policy 55, 119, 120, 129
consequence of 11
definition 2, 3, 4
development 12
ecosystem 126–32
effectiveness 45, 128
EU law 4–5
global 3
impact 7
importance of 8–9, 131
performance 5
relationship with technology policy 1, 6, 7, 11, 12, 127, 131
role in the economy 12, 45, 54, 75, 116, 124, 131
strategy 125
unintended consequences 73
institutional factors 26, 27
intellectual property 77, 79, 80, 84, 105, 106, 111, 112, 131

key performance indicators 85
knowledge transfer 93, 94, 114–15, 130, 131
KTP (Knowledge Transfer Partnership) 85

lab to market 2
legislative framework 129, 130, 131
linear model (policy paradigm) 11, 15, 24, 45, 46, 53, 75, 124, 131

marginal private cost 37, 38, 79, 86
MFP (multi-factor productivity) growth 9, 11, 24, 25, 26, 27, 28
U.K. (1985–2018) 24
U.S. (1985–2018) 25
MNC (multinational corporation) 85

National Innovation Policies: What Countries Do Best and How They Can Improve (2019) 8
NCRA (National Cooperative Research Act, 1984) 90
NIST (National Institute of Standards and Technology) 115
NRC (National Research Council) 9

objective function 52
OECD (Organisation for Economic Co-operation and Development) 4, 9, 10, 12, 16, 17, 21, 26, 31, 38, 87, 90, 118, 123, 127
oil crisis (1973) 11

patents
applications 80, 81, 82–3, 84, 114
economics of 78–80
EPO (European Patent Office) 77, 78, 80, 81, 82–3
granted 83
influence of 80
intensity of patenting 80–84
Patent Act (1790) 77
'*patents as strategic weapons*' 80
portfolio 80
protection 80
systems 76–8, 79, 80, 91
USPTO (U.S. Patent and Trademark Office) 80, 81, 82–3
policy
agency 127
ambitions 125
definition 2, 3
development 130, 131
documents 3
effectiveness 16, 45
efforts 75
enablers 130–31
environment 85
focus 125
incentives 94
instrument creators 129–30
interventions 45, 52, 85, 125, 130
makers 51, 52–4
mix 16
paradigm 11, 15, 24, 45, 53, 75, 124, 131
public 131
regulators 131
scope 130
tool 35, 38

private hurdle rate 54, 73
private sector firm 16, 37, 78, 79, 80, 107, 111, 130
  development 56
  direct subsidies 38, 40, 49
  government support 36, 39, 40, 48, 49
  investment decision-making strategy 54
  investment in R&D 17, 21, 23, 28, 30, 37, 38, 43, 53, 79
  knowledge transfer 94, 95, 111
  private hurdle rate 54, 73
  productivity growth 93
  R&D collaboration decisions 84, 90
  tax incentives 48
private-sector investments 12, 15, 16–43, 45, 46, 75, 93, 126, 128
  direct subsidy 75
  impact on technology development 76
  productivity growth 24–8
  R&D finance by country 17, 21, 22
  R&D spending by G7 firms 20
  R&D spending by U/ firms 18, 26
  R&D spending by U.S. firms 19, 26
  R&D spending in 2017 23
  rate of return 54
  risk 29–30
  tax incentives 31, 35, 75
  underinvestment in R&D 28–30
PRO (private research organization) 84
productivity growth 24–8
productivity premium 26
productivity slowdown 9–12, 40, 56, 60, 90, 111
profit-maximizing 37, 38, 72, 79, 86
Publicly Funded Research Organization 93, 115, 120
public-sector investments 15, 16, 17, 128

quadruple helix models 1, 8

R&D (research and development)
  academic sector 95–102
  allocation 7
  collaboration 12, 43, 84–91
  cost 84
  direct subsidies 38–42, 45, 46, 49, 50, 54
  financed by private sector firms 17, 21, 22, 27, 47
  government funded 100
  investment in 11, 12, 15, 28, 37, 45, 54, 55, 75, 116, 124, 126, 127
  laboratory 2, 3
  performed in G7 private sector 20
  performed in private sector in 2017 22, 23, 48, 49
  performed in the private sector 17, 21, 97
  performed in U.K. academic sector 96
  performed in U.K. private sector 18
  performed in U.S. academic sector 97
  performed in U.S. private sector 19
  policy paradigm, in the 11, 15, 24, 45, 46, 53, 75, 124, 131
  private-sector investment 16–43, 45, 46, 54, 75, 76, 93
  public sector 26, 93–116
  spending by G7 firms 20
  spending by U.K. firms 18
  spending by U.S. firms 19
  supply 7
  tax incentives 30–38, 45, 48, 50, 54
  underinvestment 28–30
R&I (research and innovation) 5
rate of return 29, 37, 38, 54, 55, 78, 79, 86, 91
recession (2007–2009) 11
recessionary period 24, 25
Regional Innovation Scorecard 5, 7
regression model 25, 26, 46, 50
research
  academic 102, 123
  applied 17, 85, 93, 95, 113
  basic 17, 26, 86, 93, 97, 99, 100
  collaboration 85, 86, 90, 102–106
  funding 40, 85
  grants 84
  industrial 122

information 84
joint venture 90, 91
organizations 84, 93, 95, 106, 130
parks 107
partnership 85
PRO (private research organization) 84
process 84
program 56, 57, 84, 85, 130, 131
progress 6
public sector 84, 93, 106, 119, 121, 130, 131
university with firm 102–6
research and technology development 5
resources 55, 129
risk 29, 30, 31

SBIR (Small Business Innovation Research) program 40, 41, 42, 50, 51
creation 57
funding patterns 57, 60–71
legislative history 55–60
Phase I 41, 42, 57–60, 61, 63–6, 68, 69, 70
Phase II 41, 42, 58–60, 62, 63–6, 67, 68–72
Phase III 58
reauthorization timeline 58–9
technology funded by 71–3
unanticipated consequences 60, 71–3
SBRI (Small Business Research Initiative) 40, 41, 42
scholarly publications 100, 101
science
definition 2, 3
NSF (National Science Foundation) 56, 57, 66, 67, 68, 71
parks 107, 108–9, 110, 111
publication of articles 101–102
Science—the Endless Frontier (1945) 11, 60
sectoral challenges 7
Small Business Innovation Development Act (1982) 40, 57, 58
SME (small and medium sized enterprises) 31, 84, 85, 89, 118
social hurdle rate 55, 73
social profit 38
social rate of return 29, 37, 38, 55
societal grand challenges 7
stakeholders 73, 85, 120, 124
Stevenson-Wydler Act (1980) 95, 115
subsidies 12, 30, 38–42, 45, 46, 49, 50, 54, 58, 75
supply-side incentives 94

target variable 15, 43, 53, 75, 93, 132
tax credit 32–34, 35, 38
tax incentives 12, 31, 45, 50, 54
advantages 35
designing 35
disadvantages 31, 35
economics of 37, 37
effectiveness 35, 45, 46
EU 31, 32–4
impacts 31
OECD Compendium of Information on R&D Tax Incentives (2019) 38
OECD R&D Tax Incentive Database (2020) 38
policy mechanism 30
private sector R&D 30–38, 46, 48, 75
U.K. 30, 38
U.S. 30, 38
technology 6, 15, 16, 29, 30, 73, 80, 83, 84, 107, 111, 119–21, 123, 129
definition 2, 3, 94
development 7, 41, 72, 75, 76, 93
funded 71, 72
patented 79, 115
policy paradigm, in the 11, 15, 24, 45, 53, 75, 124, 131
TPO (Technology Partnerships Office) 115
transfers 56, 85, 94, 95, 111, 112, 113, 114, 121, 130, 131

technology policy
 anticipated consequences 53
 barriers 29, 30
 definition 2, 3
 development 131
 direct subsidy 50, 54
 ecosystem 91, 127, 128–31
 effectiveness 11, 43, 45–51, 53, 127, 128, 129
 enablers 130–31
 environment 12, 75–91, 126, 128
 impact of 7
 implementation 7, 12, 73, 127, 128, 129, 130, 131, 132
 indirect 106
 innovation 131
 instrument creators 129–30
 intent 130
 mechanisms 30–42
 private sector 30, 115, 127
 public sector 93, 96, 113, 115, 127
 relationship with innovation policy 1, 6, 7, 11, 12, 127, 131
 research 128
 role in the economy 12, 45, 54, 75, 116, 124, 126, 131
 socially optimal 55
 strategy 125
 study of 6, 7, 8
 target variable 15
 tax incentive 54
 tools 128
 U.K. 9
 unanticipated consequences 52–73, 131
 U.S. 9, 50, 60
technology transfers 85, 94, 95, 111, 112, 113, 114, 121, 131
Treaty on the Functioning of the European Union 4, 5, 6
triple helix models 1, 8

UNESCO (United Nations Educational, Scientific and Cultural Organization) 110
University-Business Cooperation in Europe Programme 103
U.S. Domestic Policy Review (1979) 56, 57, 90

variable 25, 26, 29, 46, 50
 binary 50
 dependent 50
 independent 46, 50
 MFP (multi-factor productivity) 25
 target 15, 43, 53, 75, 93, 132